Lotteries, Schism, and Swedenborg

Lotteries, Schism, and Swedenborg

Robert Hindmarsh and the New Jerusalem Church

ANDREW HINDMARSH

WIPF & STOCK · Eugene, Oregon

LOTTERIES, SCHISM, AND SWEDENBORG
Robert Hindmarsh and the New Jerusalem Church

Wipf & Stock
An Imprint of Wipf and Stock Publishers
199 W. 8th Ave., Suite 3
Eugene, OR 97401

www.wipfandstock.com

PAPERBACK ISBN: 979-8-3852-6661-6
HARDCOVER ISBN: 979-8-3852-6662-3
EBOOK ISBN: 979-8-3852-6663-0

VERSION NUMBER 02/26/26

Engraving of Robert Hindmarsh from a painting by Joseph Allen, from the Swedenborg Society Archives. Photo: Andrew Hindmarsh.

A version of chapter 10 was originally published in the *Swedenborg Review*, 0.05, Winter 2024, as "Peterloo and the Politics of Robert Hindmarsh."

To Sarah, who first suggested writing this book and without whose endless support and tolerance of my disappearing into libraries and filling our house with copies of obscure manuscripts it would never have been written.

Contents

Preface

When you embark on a journey into family history, you never know where you might end up. You may just find endless lines of laborers or textile workers, housemaids, or mothers who left little imprint on the written record other than their births, marriages, and deaths. No doubt many were significant in their own community and their own time, but without any written records there is no way of getting behind the brief mentions in official registers. If you are lucky, however, you may turn up someone with a historical record that tells a story of who they were, what they did, and why they did it. Suddenly you have access to a personality, a character, someone you can relate to and understand.

So when I came across Robert Hindmarsh and realized he was a relation (my first cousin six times removed), he immediately piqued my interest. I delved into libraries and online resources, and the deeper I went the more interesting he became. Not only was he born in Alnwick, in the North East of England, the home of nearly all of my Hindmarsh ancestors, but like me he had had a Methodist upbringing. Unlike me he had lived in an age of religious ferment where older mystical and alchemical traditions jostled with newer rationalist ideas in a context of evangelical revivals and revolutionary thinking. Amidst all this, Robert embarked on a path towards a new form of Christianity, one based on the writings of Emanuel Swedenborg, a Swedish scientist, engineer, and civil servant turned theologian. The resulting New Church, which Robert was instrumental in bringing into being, kept records of its activities, published journals, and engaged in vigorous written debate in which Robert was a frequent contributor and sometimes the subject of debate himself. The story these records told was a fascinating one, with missing pages, shady dealings, a lost fortune, and (no protestant sect would be complete without it) arguments about sex.

But there was also a puzzle. The various characterizations of Robert in the documents were hugely variable—no one seemed to able to agree on what kind of person he was. To some he was a saint who could do no wrong, a tireless campaigner for truth; to others he was an egomaniac determined to mold the nascent New Church to his will. Then, in modern academic literature (where there is considerable interest in the origins of the New Church due to the involvement of some prominent intellectuals such as William Blake), Robert was sometimes portrayed as a dangerous subversive who tried to cover up his youthful radicalism in later life. These characterizations were so far apart that they could not all be accurate, and so trying to dig underneath them to uncover what I could of the real Robert became something of a quest. Such a quest is, of course, doomed to fail, as any account of the life of another comes from a particular perspective, and that of a family member two hundred years later has no special merit in itself. However, I tried to understand the context of the other authors and tease out where they were driven by political or doctrinal issues. I cannot claim to have written the definitive account of Robert's life, but I hope it is more balanced than some of the more transparently ideological approaches I encountered.

In preparing this book, I am particularly grateful to the Swedenborg Society in London, UK, and especially their librarian, Alex Murray. He not only let me loose in the Society's library but also helped me greatly in tracking down articles in eighteenth-century journals and obscure manuscripts that hadn't been properly catalogued. James Wilson was also very supportive and facilitated the publication of an article in the Society's magazine, which turned into one of the chapters of this book. The Queen's Foundation in Birmingham, UK, kindly gave me access to their library to read up on the theological background to the period. Clive Marsh, theologian, educator, and long-standing friend, read and commented on an early draft, which proved very helpful in shaping the final version. Then my copyeditor, Beth Gallick, with her astonishing eye for detail and always helpful suggestions, improved the manuscript immensely. And, of course, without the encouragement and support of my family, especially my wife and three daughters, it would never have seen the light of day.

Andrew Hindmarsh
Sheffield, UK, December 2025

Introduction

The history of the Priesthood of the Lord's New Church contains no name more worthy of remembrance than that of Robert Hindmarsh. The founder of the first organisation of the Church, the first receiver of her Baptism, the first ordainer of her Priesthood, the unwearied translator and publisher of her Doctrines, a hero of Michael defending her Faith against the Dragon, the deepest and soundest of her early theologians, in short, the high-priest of the Church for half a century; in all these lights Robert Hindmarsh stands forth pre-eminent in the early annals of the New Church.

CARL ODHNER, *ROBERT HINDMARSH: A BIOGRAPHY*

ACCOLADES DO NOT COME much more effusive than that one, in a biography by Carl Odhner, published in 1895 (though a Lancashire printer, John Grundy, did go so far as to name one of his children Robert Hindmarsh Grundy). But if it all sounds more like hagiography than biography, James Hyde, a New Church historian, would agree:

> The biography of Robert Hindmarsh that will satisfy the discriminating student of New Church history, has not been written. . . . [Odhner's biography] shows no sense of proportion, no historic perspective: it magnifies the insignificant, and belittles the worthy; it paints the subject's errors as his great achievements; it guesses where it should either hold reserved silence, or seek out the facts; and above all it sees the variable and human subject as an infallible and hierarchical monitor—mistaking the transitory for the permanent. As a contribution to a genuine history of the New

> Church, and an estimate of its place in general history, it is . . . of small value.[1]

Hyde, both here and elsewhere, tends towards the opposite extreme, never hesitating to identify errors or fallibility and painting a picture of Robert as a flawed human being with an inability to see any views other than his own. Other writers also reflect this polarized view of him, suggesting humility, charity, and piety "were not particularly conspicuous"[2] in his life, or alternatively that he was "as true a man as ever trod this godly earth."[3] There is clearly space for a new assessment of Robert's life that might make some sense of these diverse interpretations.

Robert Hindmarsh was born in Alnwick, Northumberland, in 1759, was educated in Bristol, worked as a printer and then a failed stockbroker in London, and finally was a preacher and pastor in Salford, Manchester. While Odhner's characterization of him might be suspect, he does correctly identify him, alongside his other activity, as an important figure in the development of the New Jerusalem Church. This was a church based on the teachings of Emanuel Swedenborg (1688–1772), a Swedish scientist, engineer, and civil servant who turned theologian when he started having experiences in which he believed he had entered the spiritual realm and received a new revelation. Swedenborg was one of the many and diverse thinkers in the eighteenth century as the new rationalism of Descartes, Locke, and others jostled with older mystical traditions for the attention of those seeking enlightenment. In some thirty books written between 1749 and 1771 he set out this new revelation at great length and in great detail. While Swedenborg is often described as a mystic, based on his accounts of entering the spiritual world and talking with angels, his writings are not typical of mystics, as in style and approach they are more reflective of his early life as a scientist and engineer. This gave them a logic and coherence that perhaps appealed to the more rational eighteenth-century minds than the more obviously mystical thinkers.

Swedenborg strongly asserted the unity of God, with the Father (love), the Son (wisdom), and the Holy Spirit (activity) being a trinity of qualities of God, reflected in the human soul, body, and mind. All of creation had its origins in the divine love and wisdom, and so all created things in the material world correspond to spiritual realities. The true and proper order

1. Hyde, "Some Notes I," 65–66.
2. Barrett, *Catholicity*, 264.
3. Mason, "Letter," 188.

of things had been disturbed by the misuse of human free will, so God came into the world in material form as Jesus. During his life he resisted every possible temptation and lived to the full the true nature of God. In doing so, by resisting all temptation, Jesus broke the power of evil spirits, and through his example all people can achieve a similar harmony between their spiritual and material nature. Redemption was not achieved through the sacrifice on the cross, but in providing a power to enable people to improve themselves. Those who show by the way they live their lives that they truly desire to be saved, will be saved. Swedenborg claimed to have witnessed the last judgment in one of his visits to the spiritual realm in 1757, and the result of this was that influxes from the spiritual realm were renewing the natural realm through an inner and spiritual second coming of Jesus.

Swedenborg thus developed a systematic worldview, based firmly within Christianity but differing from orthodox Christianity in a number of fundamental respects, notably his interpretation of the Trinity and of salvation. This meant he was rejected by most contemporaries and the mainstream churches, and indeed was frequently the object of ridicule. John Wesley went so far as to accuse him of insanity.[4] However, there were some who greeted his ideas with enthusiasm and some of them went on to found a New Church. It was here that Robert Hindmarsh came to prominence as a leading advocate of Swedenborgianism and a driving force behind the formation of the New Church, earning thereby his entry in the British *Dictionary of National Biography*.[5]

The New Church did not have an easy birth. There were many among the followers of Swedenborg who didn't think it should exist at all, and among those that did there were disputes about where a priesthood might come from, about the role of a priesthood in church government, and about matters of doctrine. In all these disputes Robert played a leading role, often supporting a quite extreme position. He was a strong supporter of the foundation of the New Church, a strong advocate for a priesthood, and a proponent of views regarding marriage that others condemned. He was continually among a minority, expelled on one occasion, and left in a tiny group when the majority up and left. And yet he remained a fervent supporter of Swedenborg and a central figure in the church, in later life

4. Tafel, *Documents*, 582.

5. Lineham, "Hindmarsh."

becoming a minister to a congregation in Salford and a regular president of its annual conferences.

A study of the life of Robert Hindmarsh not only gives insight into the character of a leading and controversial figure in the life of the New Church, but also gives some insight into the development of the church itself. Despite its unorthodoxy (from the point of view of the mainstream churches of the time) the New Church did not exist in a vacuum, and many of its concerns and controversies reflected the theological and ecclesiastical context of the times. Garrett's assessment was that "among all the eighteenth-century religious movements that generated a millenarian sensibility on the eve of the French Revolution, the most important was probably the Church of the New Jerusalem,"[6] and so understanding the origins of the New Church helps to illuminate the broader religious trends of the time. Similarly, those broader religious trends help to illuminate the life of Robert Hindmarsh.

6. Garrett, *Respectable Folly*, 155.

I

Alnwick and Bristol

One day, around 1744, John Trembath rode into Alnwick, a small market town in Northumberland, the most northerly county in England. He stood at the foot of Clayport Street, just off the Market Place, and began to preach. Trembath was one of John Wesley's early assistants and brought with him the wave of evangelical preaching that Wesley and others were spreading across eighteenth-century England. After that first occasion he preached every fortnight standing on a horse block in front of an old thatched public house at the bottom of the Market Place. Among the crowds who gathered there each fortnight was William Hindmarsh, a young tanner working in his father's business and already, at the age of just thirty, a member of the ruling council of freemen in the town, and one of the overseers of the poor. He lived at the bottom of Clayport Street and could probably have heard Trembath from his house on at least that first occasion.

Trembath preached with great eloquence and zeal,[1] and there was a growing Methodist society by the time of John Wesley's first visit to Alnwick in 1748. William's younger brother James, who turned twelve years old in 1744 and would become Robert Hindmarsh's father fifteen years later, may well have come with William to hear Trembath too, but if not at such a young age, then almost certainly soon after. Both William and James were among the early converts to Methodism in Alnwick.[2]

1. Stanley, "Memoir," 794.
2. Tate, *History*, 195.

William took over the family tanning business after his father died and became a prominent citizen in Alnwick, rising to the office of chamberlain, one of the four leading freemen, and eventually passed a successful business on to his eldest son. He was probably not a particularly prominent Methodist as, while there are few early records, he does not appear in a list of class leaders compiled around 1757 and he still maintained private seatings in the parish church at the time of his will.[3]

William's younger brother and Robert's father, James, however, was a rather different character. He too became a freeman, but he either had no interest in the family business or there was no room for him. He was also a much more unsettled character, veering about between occupations and religious affiliations as he sought a place in the world. He started out as a barber and wigmaker but gave this up to try innkeeping, placing regular advertisements between October 1760 and May 1761 in the *Caledonian Mercury* and *Newcastle Courant* for the newly refurbished Red Lion in Alnwick. This may have been unsuccessful, or perhaps he identified a better business opportunity, because in May 1762 he took over the inn at Beltenford, near Dunbar, just over the border in Scotland, and started advertising that. This was a substantial property (he paid window tax on eighteen windows) and he tried to encourage clientele by pointing out that the road through Beltenford had been improved and it would be cheaper taking a coach that way rather than the main road through Dunbar. This enterprise was definitely unsuccessful, leaving numerous debts in its wake, and it was not until 1799 (by which time James was sixty-seven years old) that a meeting of his creditors in a village near Dunbar were finally paid what had been recovered from the venture.[4]

James was an enthusiastic Methodist, but this initial zeal faded about the time he took up innkeeping,[5] and he fell away from the new Methodist movement before returning a few years later in penitence:

> Being a man of considerable ability, Mr. Hindmarsh was able to render good service to the great founder of Methodism in gathering together, under the shadow of Alnwick Castle, an active and zealous body of worshippers. Among the leading spirits of the

3. For more details of the family background, see Hindmarsh, *History of the Hindmarshes*.

4. Anon., "To Hindmarsh's Creditors," 1.

5. Methodism did not become opposed to alcohol until the temperance movement of the nineteenth century.

> little flock he held a useful and prominent place. After a time, his ardour cooled. Becoming a publican, first at the Castle Inn, Alnwick, and then at a similar house in Dunbar, he gradually "fell away" from the Methodist society, and either resigned or was deprived of the privileges of its communion. Both his innkeeping enterprises proved unsuccessful. After his failure at Dunbar, he returned to his native town, and, under the depressing influences of commercial disaster, sought consolation among the friends he had forsaken. Mr. Wesley, satisfied with his proofs of repentance, and convinced of his competency to teach and preach, appointed him governor of Kingswood School, near Bath, and admitted him into the ministry.[6]

John Wesley, the leader of the Methodist movement, appointed James as chief English and mathematical master at Kingswood School in 1765, a school near Bristol that had been founded by Wesley for the children of local colliers but that was increasing taking the sons of itinerant Methodist ministers. His wife was appointed housekeeper, and so James and Phyllis took their children on the long journey from Alnwick to Bristol. Wesley thereby not only gave James a new and settled purpose to his life, but also a useful distance from his creditors.

Robert, the youngest of the four children, had been born in Alnwick on November 8, 1759, and so he was aged six when he became a pupil at Kingswood School along with his elder brother John (but not his two sisters, as it was a school for boys).[7] He acquired there a proficiency in Latin and Greek, suggesting that he followed the more academic curriculum offered by the school. This included Latin, Greek, Hebrew, French, numerous classical authors such as Plato, Euclid, Homer, Livy, Suetonius and Tacitus, Shakespeare, Milton, Newton, and Locke. Wesley commented that "whoever goes carefully through this course, will be a better scholar than nine in ten of the graduates at Oxford or Cambridge."[8] Whether that is true is hard to say (though Wesley spoke from experience as a student and subsequently fellow at Oxford) but Robert undoubtedly left the school with a wide-ranging education. His knowledge of Latin in particular, the language of Swedenborg's books, would become significant in his later life. An eagerness to study never left him, and he was said to have "borrowed . . . many

6. Welford, *Men of Mark*, 528–29. The reference to the Castle Inn is probably a mistake given the newspaper adverts placed by James were for the Red Lion.

7. Three Old Boys, register for 1748–1897 in *History of Kingswood School*, 56.

8. Wesley, *Short Account*, 12.

hours from the night"[9] in study as his business occupied him during the day. He would read Swedenborg in the original Latin and take books to bed with him, often reading until he fell asleep (a rather dangerous habit in the era of candles).

After a few years at Kingswood school, Robert, by this time aged nine, became caught up in a religious revival among the boys, in which his father played a leading role. In April 1768 James wrote about it to Wesley:

> Reverend and Dear Sir, On Wednesday, the 20th, God broke in upon our boys in a surprising manner. A serious concern has been observable in some of them for some time past. But that night, while they were in their private apartments, the power of God came upon them, even like a mighty rushing wind, which made them cry aloud for mercy. Last night, I hope, will never be forgotten, when about twenty were in the utmost distress. But God quickly spoke peace to two of them, J[ohn] Gl[asco]t and T[homas] M[auric]e. A greater display of his love I never saw: they indeed rejoice with joy unspeakable. For my own part, I have not often felt the like power. We have no need to exhort them to pray, for that spirit runs through the whole school, so that this house may well be called a house of prayer. While I am writing, the cries of the boys from their several apartments are sounding in my ears. . . . Since I began to write, eight more are set at liberty and now rejoice in God their Saviour. The names of these are John Coward, John Lyon, John Maddern, John Boddily, John Thurgar, Charles Brown, William Higham, and Robert Hindmarsh. Their age is from eight to fourteen.[10]

Wesley, when he visited Kingswood a few months later, pronounced that he had "spent an hour, much to my satisfaction with the boys at Kingswood . . . all behave in a manner that I have seen no other schoolboys like them."[11] The climax of the revival came two years later in 1770 after the boys had been taken to see the body of a neighbor who had died. James gave them "an exhortation suited to the occasion" and there were "strong cries and tears till about nine o'clock."[12] Ten days later, the boys were sent to bed, but three of them, including Robert, "resolved they would not sleep, nor rest, till God revealed himself to them." And so it went on, with much

9. Noble, *Sermon*, 7.

10. Wesley, *Journal*, 325–26.

11. Wesley, *Journal*, 351.

12. Wesley, *Journal*, 420.

weeping and praying, exhortations from the masters, and involving the maids at the school as well as the boys. One morning James was awoken between four and five in the morning by the children "vehemently crying to God," in which they were joined by the maids. One boy refused all food "but remained in words or groans calling upon God."[13]

Wesley regarded it all as a "wonderful work of grace" and was greatly disappointed to find that the effects had all vanished by September 1771. Later commentators were less charitable, describing James as

> a man of the most dangerous evangelistic type, in whom was concentrated all that emotional hysteria which is so often the cause of religious "revivals." . . . [He was one of a group of] misguided fanatics . . . who, carried away by an ignorant evangelical enthusiasm, were continually working upon the emotional forces of their hearers, and who mistook this appalling breakdown of rational control, which bordered on common hysteria, for the outpouring of the Holy Spirit upon men—a latter-day Pentecost. Hindmarsh, Rankin and Mather [two other masters who were involved] were men of this type and . . . can be regarded as the real cause of the revivals.[14]

The masters were "these insane persons" in the context of events that were "worthy of Bedlam, and might fairly have entitled the promoters to a place there."[15] Though to be fair to James and the others, many Methodist societies were caught up in a wave of emotion around that time, so the boys were reflecting what was happening around them, and Wesley himself had told his preachers that children should be instructed in earnest.[16]

The effect of all this on Robert is hard to gauge. While it might appear to show early signs of the religious zeal he came to show later, he never refers to it in all his writings. This may mean the impact was limited or that he regarded it as the naïve enthusiasm of children who didn't understand what they were doing, egged on by the adults. It might even have had a negative impact, making Robert wary of the more emotional aspects of the evangelical revival and its expression in Methodism, which in turn might explain the fact that he never joined the church in which his father was so

13. Wesley, *Journal*, 422–23.

14. Body, *John Wesley and Education*, 119–25.

15. Southey, *Life of Wesley*, 509.

16. Ives, *Kingswood School*, 63.

involved. However, growing up in such a strongly religious environment fits with his later expressed desire for religious understanding and truth.

James was appointed an itinerant preacher in 1771, though it was not until two years later that he took up itinerancy and left Kingswood to serve successively in Wiltshire, Devon, London, Leeds, Keighley, Bradford, Canterbury, and Norwich. Itinerant preachers were one of the two types of preacher in Methodism at the time: *itinerant* preachers were appointed and sent by the annual Methodist Conference to lead Methodism in a particular place, usually a new place every year; *local* preachers retained their homes and professions but led Methodist worship on at least some Sundays in their local area. James could be an inspiring preacher, as when George Osborn, a prominent early Methodist in Kent, went to hear him at the local chapel:

> The sermon which first aroused his more serious attention was preached by Mr James Hindmarsh, second Preacher at Canterbury in 1781. . . . The scope of the sermon was to expose the folly of those persons who constantly used the Liturgy of the Established Church, and yet were strangers, and perhaps enemies, to vital godliness.[17]

In 1777 there occurred another significant event in Robert's childhood: the death of his elder sister Elizabeth when he was seventeen years old and she was just twenty. The British Library contains no less than eleven copies of the pamphlet *A Short Account of the Death of Elizabeth Hindmarsh*, which describes her last hours in great detail. At least four editions were published, and versions were printed in London, Leeds, and Manchester.

The deathbed narrative was popularized during the evangelical revival of the eighteenth century, becoming particularly prevalent in Victorian times, but it has its roots in earlier Puritanism and the concern for the fate of the soul. For Protestant evangelicals, the doctrine of justification by grace through faith meant that living a good life was insufficient for salvation, so there was a natural focus on the state of the soul at death. Methodists in particular tended to look to feelings and a specific assurance of salvation. The resulting events were then frequently written up as a test of piety, a display of the power and grace of God, which would encourage others in their faith.[18]

Elizabeth was born in Alnwick on May 20, 1757, the second child of James and Phyllis. The pamphlet says she

17. JMH, "Methodism in Kent," 581–82.

18. Rack, "Evangelical Endings."

> was sent early to school, and was very early instructed by her parents in the principles of religion. Hence she was remarkably obedient to them, and blameless in her behaviour.[19]

Then, in February 1777, while James was stationed in London, Elizabeth fell ill with tuberculosis, and by May it was clear she was unlikely to live much longer. In early July she was moved to Kingswood School where Cornelius Bayley, one of the masters there and the author of the pamphlet at the request of James, took a careful pastoral interest in her. It isn't clear why she moved to Bristol, but her mother (though not any of her brothers and sisters) was present at the end, and so she probably traveled there with her. It may have been thought that the location of the school would be better for her health, and her parents' connections with Kingswood enabled her to go there.

Early in September,

> she fell into a fit which she took to be a sign of her approaching dissolution. And now her excessive fears began. She cried aloud. She wept bitterly. She prayed with all her might, seeing the king of terrors advance with hasty strides. The curtain was now drawn aside, and she saw eternity without a covering. She trembled at the thought of meeting an angry God, and of having her doom fixt for ever. . . .
>
> Before the clock struck ten, the Lord drew near, and satisfied the desire of her longing soul. She was filled with love, joy and peace in believing: yea her cup ran over. She could now look with composure on death, judgement, and eternity; yea and rejoice at their approach, She grieved no more at the loss of health, friends, or all the world!
>
> Till the Lord manifested himself unto her, she was full of pain and anguish: she could not bear to be moved in her bed, or even to be touched with a finger. But as soon as he appeared, she broke out into holy rapture, such as no tongue can speak. She cried, "Happy, happy, happy! I feel no pain now! I am quite well! O sweet Jesus! I am going to heaven." . . .
>
> "Write," said she, "to my father, and tell him I shall be happy; tell him I am happy. Tell him I am going to Jesus, where I hope to see him very soon."[20]

19. Bayley, *Short Account*, 3.
20. Bayley, *Short Account*, 5–8.

The account continues in this vein for several pages, with Elizabeth having another phase of doubt and fear before once again proclaiming herself to be happy. At one point there was a sound in her throat and she asked if it was "what is commonly called the rattles? How long does it come before death?" By noon the following day "she was scarce able to speak."

> About three, a friend coming into the room, she looked at him with smiling countenance, and said, "O, I am happy! I shall not long be here: I shall soon be in paradise." Not long after, she whispered to her mother, "I shall be in paradise quickly." She then drew her breath once or twice, and expired without a groan.[21]

Thus ended the short life of Elizabeth Hindmarsh. She did not have time to achieve much, even if the social environment of the late eighteenth century would have allowed it, but her last days were turned into a morally uplifting tract in the style of the times, and so she achieved a certain immortality that way. Robert is not mentioned as having been present at her death (by this time he was an apprentice printer in London), and once again Robert does not mention the events in his writings. However, it does reinforce the picture of a pious evangelical family background surrounding him while growing up.

A few years later and James was starting to tire of being a Methodist preacher. Robert had first become interested in the writings of Emanuel Swedenborg in January 1782 while visiting his father (of which much more later), and James clearly became interested around the same time. Thomas Cooper, a minister appointed to preach in Norwich along with James in August 1782, complained that he had to work hard "amidst great discouragements" because his superintendent minister, James, hardly ever came by and had "imbibed the strange and cursory views of Baron Swedenborg."[22]

In 1783 James was sufficiently dissatisfied with Methodism to resign as an itinerant preacher. He went to live in Great Yarmouth where he had many friends who were familiar with his preaching and who wanted him to preach there every week. This upset one of the local Methodist preachers, a Mr. King, who found much of his congregation would leave if he was found to be in the pulpit. John Wesley himself was needed to settle the dispute, and he secured agreement with the Methodist society to allow Mr. King to preach there once a month, but he had very small congregations. Part

21. Bayley, *Short Account*, 12.

22. Cooper, "Memoir," 81.

of the reason for the dispute was probably that the supporters of Mr. King doubted James's attachment to the Methodist cause.[23]

Also around this time, James Hindmarsh was associated with the Countess of Huntingdon's Connexion, a Calvinist evangelical society supported by the countess, but in keeping with his general inability to stick with anything for more than a few years, he deserted it in order to become the "High Priest of the Society of Swedenborgians."[24] These incidents all suggest a picture of James as dissatisfied with Methodism and searching for an alternative, but he did not settle upon Swedenborg and join his son until around 1785,[25] after which his story becomes bound up with that of Robert.

One final anecdote from this pre-Swedenborgian period in James's life: While he was a Methodist preacher in Wiltshire he met and became great friends with Isaac Hawkins, a local preacher there, and the friendship lasted for the rest of their lives. When James embraced the Swedenborgians he immediately met with Isaac (who by now was living in London) to share his good news. Isaac embraced them too, and this resulted in him being hauled before Wesley and a number of his leading preachers to be cross-examined. This in turn led to Isaac's expulsion from the Methodist connexion, though Wesley himself opposed it on the grounds that no one whose life was good should be expelled.[26] Later Isaac, along with James, became one of the first Swedenborgian preachers, and expulsions such as this probably influenced the formation of the New Jerusalem Church.

James died in Keighley in 1812 at the age of eighty. His eldest daughter, Hannah, had married William Illingworth, and they both lived there (they had probably met when James was stationed in Keighley as a Methodist preacher); it was probably in their home where James died, as William was present at the end. According to Robert, "his last illness . . . appear[ed] to have been the effect of a decay of nature, rather than of any particular disorder."[27]

Robert was thus born into a world of small businesses in a remote market town. Alnwick was thirty-four miles from Newcastle, some four

23. Watmough, *History of Methodism*, 84–89.

24. Anon., *Pre-Existence*, 39. See also Rowell, *Note on the History*, 11. Rowell thought this was an error and should have referred to Robert, but the Countess's Connexion was only formed in 1783 after Robert started a Swedenborgian group in London, and so the timing doesn't work for him.

25. Hindmarsh, "Death of Mr James," 220.

26. Sibly, "Obituary," 265.

27. Hindmarsh, "Death of Mr James," 221.

hours by coach (for those who could afford it), and the best part of two days by coach from London. Clever young men could be successful in business in Alnwick, become reasonably wealthy, and, if they were freemen, be leaders in local government, which is what Robert's Hindmarsh relatives did until the early twentieth century. However, to have a wider impact on the world it would be necessary to leave, and here the character of his father played an important role. James struggled in business, completely failing as an innkeeper, and it was only when Wesley recognized the abilities he did have and sent him to Kingswood that he became more settled and achieved a clearer role in life (notwithstanding his somewhat dubious role in the revival at the school).

This proved to be the making of Robert. While the Alnwick freemen were commendably supportive of education, he received a far more extensive education at Kingswood than he would have done at one of the schools in Alnwick. Then, in 1773, at the age of about fourteen, he was taken out of school and placed by his parents as an apprentice to a printer, Joseph Fry, in Worship Street, London. This coincided with James becoming an itinerant preacher, and so the timing may be associated with that. While becoming an apprentice in an artisan trade might seem a continuation of the world of small business he left behind in Alnwick, it in fact opened up the eighteenth century to him. London was a city alive with competing ideas and philosophies, and printing put him in contact with people participating in the intellectual and religious life of Europe.

Thus, while Robert grew up in a pious, evangelical family, steeped in the conservative non-conformism of John Wesley, being taken to Bristol expanded his horizons beyond the isolated market town in Northumberland where he was born, and his Kingswood education taught him the language and ideas of eighteenth-century intellectual life. He might have been an apprentice to a trade, but the foundations were there for an altogether larger role in London life.

2

London and Swedenborg

ROBERT BECAME AN APPRENTICE printer in 1773, but it is less clear why he chose printing or the firm of Joseph Fry. Printing was a growth industry at the time, following the removal of press regulation at the end of the seventeenth century and the increasing numbers of newspapers and printed pamphlets, which may have made it an attractive business to join. The link into the intellectual world of books and ideas may also have been attractive to Robert or his parents, who presumably recognized his academic ability, but none of this is certain. There is a link, however, to Joseph Fry, as he was originally based in Bristol and so James Hindmarsh may have encountered him there. Fry began as a doctor but abandoned medicine to set up a business making chocolate (a business eventually taken over by Cadbury, but the name still survives in the chocolate bar Fry's Chocolate Cream). He then became interested in printing and went into partnership with the printer of the *Bristol Gazette* before moving the operation to London around 1770, where he printed a number of Wesley's works. Fry was not a Methodist, and his children are not listed as having attended Kingswood School,[1] but it is possible that he and James knew each other in Bristol or that the printing provided a link with Methodism and a reason for Robert to be placed there.

As a young apprentice Robert lodged with Josiah Collier, a Quaker who was also a partner in Fry's printing firm, and they would often meet and talk with another Quaker printer and friend of the Collier family, James

1. Three Old Boys, *History of Kingswood School.*

Phillips. This led in 1778 to Robert's first encounter with Swedenborg's writings: Phillips printed a translation of Swedenborg's *Treatise on Heaven and Hell* that year and it became a frequent topic of conversation at the dinner table. Robert did not immediately regard the book as significant but was passionately interested in religion, as he wrote in his autobiographical history *Rise and Progress of the New Jerusalem Church*:

> Observing the divisions which obtained in the Christian Church, I was anxious to acquire a knowledge of the truth, but was determined to unite myself with no sect or party, until I had made a full examination of the various doctrines taught, and compared them with the Sacred Scriptures: for these I believed to contain a revelation from heaven, though capable of an unjust or just interpretation, according to the different states of illumination with different readers.[2]

Robert makes no mention of worshiping with any particular congregation at this time (despite his upbringing, he never became a Methodist),[3] and this would fit with his statement about not uniting himself with any sect or party. Indeed Robert attended a variety of congregations in his pursuit of a "full examination of the various doctrines taught," but there was one particular theological issue that was important for him:

> I was particularly desirous of understanding the nature of the Divine Trinity; for which purpose I read many authors, and heard many preachers, of different denominations, yet without obtaining from any or all of them anything like a satisfactory or rational solution of the subject. In my estimation it appeared contradictory to assert, that Three Divine Persons have existed from eternity, each of whom singly and by himself is God and Lord, and yet that there are not Three Gods and Lords, but only One! Neither was it enough to be told, that it was a great mystery, incapable of being explained or rationally understood, and that therefore it must be implicitly believed without further inquiry.[4]

He describes in a mocking tone how he saw the doctrine as taught by the church:

> It was further considered, that these Three Divine Persons, particularly the two first of them, are described sometimes of one mind

2. Hindmarsh, *Rise and Progress*, 9.
3. Noble, *Sermon*, 6.
4. Hindmarsh, *Rise and Progress*, 9.

> and disposition, and at other times of contrary dispositions; the First Divine Person, or Father, being naturally vindictive, yet after much difficulty, suffering himself to be appeased by the sight of blood drawn from an innocent Victim; the Second Person, or Son, being in his own nature merciful, and therefore offering himself as that innocent Victim . . . ; and the Third Person, or Holy Ghost, being in the above respects altogether neutral, yet ready on all occasions to execute the designs and purposes of the other two, as soon as ever they are agreed upon.[5]

Robert was far from alone in having trouble with the doctrine of the Trinity, as it had been a source of controversy throughout the history of Christianity.[6] For the early theologians of the church the notion of one God was fundamental, but their doctrine of salvation demanded a fully divine Christ who was nonetheless distinct from God the Father. Furthermore, the various threefold characterizations of God in the Bible[7] demanded the inclusion of the Holy Spirit within the same understanding of God. This led to the difficult problem of finding a way to state how there could be both a single God and yet three distinct persons (God the Father, Son, and Holy Spirit) within that single God. The problem was later compounded by the original Greek words used to express the doctrine being translated into Latin and then local languages, which could subtly change the concepts being expressed and make the whole idea sound even more self-contradictory.

The orthodox formula for the Trinity was contained in the Nicene Creed: "Jesus Christ, the only-begotten Son of God, begotten of the Father before all worlds, Light of Light, very God of very God, begotten, not made, consubstantial with the Father."[8] It had been agreed upon at the Council of Nicaea in the year 325 and amended in 381 and had itself grown out of a major controversy over Arianism, whose central idea (rejected in the creed) was that the Son (i.e., Jesus Christ) was subordinate to the Father (i.e., God). Another major controversy, this time over the word *filioque* (meaning "and the son"), which was added to some Latin versions of the Nicene Creed a couple of hundred years later to declare that the Holy Spirit proceeded from the Father *and* the Son, was a significant factor in the split of the western, Roman church from the eastern, Orthodox church.

5. Hindmarsh, *Rise and Progress*, 51.
6. See, for example, Collins, *Trinity*; Lehner, "Trinity"; Lucci, "Reassessing the Crisis."
7. For example, Matt 28:19 and 2 Cor 13:14.
8. Church of England, *Book of Common Prayer*, 146.

The Reformation created new problems with its emphasis on Scripture, rather than the church, as the source of doctrinal authority. While there are various statements in the Bible that can be construed as pointing towards, or compatible with, the traditional doctrine of the Trinity, it is certainly not clearly stated there, and so identifying a scriptural foundation to the doctrine became problematic. A further difficulty was the developing rationalism associated with the Enlightenment, which found appeals to mystery (as a way of defending the Trinity by avoiding addressing the apparent contradiction) unconvincing. All these problems and trends had a tendency to push theologians towards either unitarianism, in which the Son and Holy Spirit are in some way subordinate to God the Father, or modalism, in which a single God has three modes of being that are not fully distinct persons.

The church, of course, resisted all these moves away from traditional orthodoxy. In England, a seventeenth-century controversy over unitarian views even led to an Act of Parliament, the Blasphemy Act of 1696. Outside the Church of England, the Presbyterians split into traditional and unitarian strands in 1719, and a growing sympathy for unitarian views led to the creation of the first avowedly unitarian congregation in London in 1774.

Given this background, it is not at all surprising that Robert (and, indeed, many others) had difficulty accepting the traditional doctrine. His statements, above, allude to several of the key issues: the relationship to Scripture, the desire for rational understanding, and the unconvincing nature of an appeal to mystery. Samuel Noble, an early Swedenborgian minister, had similar difficulties. He recalled when, in his own spiritual journey, he had been "intensely anxious upon the all-important subject of religion" for several years and commented specifically on the Trinity:

> I know by experience, what the effect is, upon truly serious minds, of entertaining an idea of more Divine Persons than one, and that, calling them one as they may, a plurality of persons cannot be distinguished in the mind from a plurality of gods.[9]

And some years later, in 1799, two American Methodist preachers cited the doctrine of the Trinity as the primary reason for resigning from the Episcopal Methodist Church.[10]

Robert continued his own account of his developing thinking:

9. Noble, *Case of Entrance*, 10.

10. Fonerden and Hargrove, "Valedictory Address," 7–8.

> I came at length to this conclusion, That there is and can only be One God in One Divine Person, and that the Lord Jesus Christ is that God. Yet, as mention is repeatedly made, in the Sacred Scriptures, of the Father, the Son, and the Holy Spirit, it appeared most evident, that something of Triplicity is compatible with the Divine Unity: and the only way on which I could at that time reconcile the apparent incongruity, was by considering, that the One God is called the Father by virtue of his being the Creator; the Son, by virtue of his being the Redeemer; and the Holy Spirit, by virtue of his being the Regenerator and Comforter of his people: thus, that there was not Three Divine Persons in the Godhead, but Three Divine Characters uniting in the person of Jesus Christ alone.[11]

Thus Robert's thinking moved in the modalist, rather than the unitarian, direction, in which a unitary God has three modes of being or operation. It also locates Robert clearly within the post-Reformation emphasis on Scripture alongside a post-Enlightenment use of reason to come to an understanding of what Scripture means. He comments that his new understanding was not sufficiently correct but that it prepared him to receive the truth he found in the works of Swedenborg.

Swedenborg himself had also found that reflection on the traditional doctrine inevitably led him to three persons, each of whom is singly God, and that therefore there are three Gods. In order to preserve the unity of God he stated that the Father, Son, and Holy Spirit are three essentials in the one God, which together make one essence. He argued that the true spiritual sense of the words "Father," "Son," and "Holy Ghost" were (as revealed by his science of correspondences) the three divine essential principles—divine love, divine wisdom, and divine proceeding power—which corresponded to the soul, body and mental operation in humans. This is arguably also a modalist form of understanding of the Trinity and probably helped to make it attractive to Robert.

On January 1, 1782, four years after his first encounter with Swedenborg, Robert was visiting his father, James, who was then living in Canterbury as a Methodist preacher, and they talked about Swedenborg's writings. James said that he knew a Quaker in the city, a George Keen, who had copies of some of them and that he would be willing to lend them to Robert. The next day, Robert borrowed two of them—*Treatise on the Nature of Influx* and *Treatise on Heaven and Hell*—and the impact was profound:

11. Hindmarsh, *Rise and Progress*, 9–10.

> These works I read with the utmost avidity, and instantly perceived their contents to be of heavenly origin. I therefore naturally embraced and delighted in them, as the eye embraces and delights in objects that reflect the golden rays of the rising sun.[12]

The appeal of *Heaven and Hell* is often attributed to the fact that it deals with life after death[13] and does so in a way that (just like Swedenborg's view of the Trinity) is quite different from that which Robert and others would have encountered elsewhere. Traditional Christianity was very definite about the existence of life after death but rather vague about what kind of life awaited the righteous (though perhaps rather more concrete about the torments awaiting the damned). Swedenborg, in claiming to have experienced heavenly life for himself, was able to give a much more definite account and one that was much closer to life on earth. The angels, who had not existed from eternity but had previously lived on earth, did not have an ethereal existence but played, worked, ate, and slept, living a real life but in a spiritual world and body. Furthermore, God was not an angry God who punishes—the spirits of people who have died are judged, but they then gravitate towards those who are like themselves, whether that be in heaven or hell.

It is possible to imagine someone in the late eighteenth century who struggled with aspects of traditional Christianity and who sought a reasoned religion finding Swedenborg very appealing. He provided a coherent theological framework that seemed to solve a number of theological conundrums, had a rather softer and less threatening view of salvation, and gave a clear account of what was in store for the righteous. His system of correspondences provided an enigmatic but, for those with skill and judgment, a rational approach to biblical interpretation. Despite the air of mysticism around Swedenborg's visions, his was a fundamentally rationalist approach that felt very different to the fanaticism and emotion of many evangelical movements.

It was not an easy step to embrace Swedenborg, as it required the rejection of traditional Christianity and the ridicule of the majority, but once embraced, it could comfortably be lived with. Curiously, the two works of Swedenborg that Robert says opened his eyes make virtually no mention at all of the doctrine of the Trinity. This suggests that resolving the problem of the Trinity, despite its foregrounding by Robert in his memoir, was not

12. Hindmarsh, *Rise and Progress*, 10–11.

13. For example, Sigstedt, *Swedenborg Epic*, 265.

important in his initial reception of Swedenborg, though it may well have become much more significant for him later.

On the same day that he borrowed those works of Swedenborg, Keen introduced Robert to Sarah Paramor, the eldest daughter of Henry Paramor, and they were married in Canterbury on May 7 that same year.

On his return to London, Robert immediately set about trying to find others who had been similarly struck by Swedenborg's writings, but he was initially disappointed:

> I expected at first, that almost every person of sound judgement, or even of common sense, would receive them with the same facility as I did myself and would rejoice with me, that so great a treasure had at length been found in the Church. But I was mistaken: and such was the prejudice in the minds of men of apparent candour in other respects, that so far from congratulating me, and their own good fortune, in the acquisition of such spiritual information, I was absolutely laughed at, and set down by them as a mere simpleton, an infatuated youth, and little better than a madman, led away by the reveries of an old enthusiast and imposter. I heard these vituperations with surprise, and could not help thinking, in return, that the accusers were themselves mad, or at least under the influence of a strong delusion.
>
> Even my own father at this time, and for two or three years after my reception of the new doctrines, cautioned me to beware how I gave way to them, that I should be seduced by mere flights of imagination, and estranged from the common faith of professing Christians.[14]

During the course of the following year, Robert managed to find a few others who shared his interest and conviction, and in 1783 they began meeting regularly at his home in Clerkenwell Close, London. In December they decided to advertise a public meeting at the London Coffee House on Ludgate Hill on December 5, 1783, which resulted in two more recruits to the cause. A few weeks later they obtained rooms in the Middle Temple and took the name Theosophical Society,[15] meeting on Thursday evenings and subsequently Sundays and Thursdays. They would read Swedenborg's works, sometimes in Latin, and discuss their meaning and significance.

14. Hindmarsh, *Rise and Progress*, 11–12.

15. Theosophy, from the Greek for wisdom of God, was originally used in the early church as a synonym for theology, but was revived in the seventeenth century, notably in its use by the German mystic Jacob Boehme (1575–1624) who influenced many millenarian movements.

Robert was just twenty-four years old but already showing a drive to put his religious views into action.

Others too were developing an interest in Swedenborg at that time. For example, Jacob Duché (who had read the opening prayer at the first congress of the USA in 1776, but was later forced to flee when suspected of English sympathy) held Sunday services at the London Asylum for Female Orphans. He was appointed chaplain there in 1783, but it is likely that he only became openly Swedenborgian around 1785. From this time the services were strongly influenced by Swedenborg and attracted many members of the Theosophical Society and others interested in the same approach.

Robert's group was thus tapping into an existing but unorganized interest in Swedenborg's works that itself reflected the broader religious and philosophical environment of the time. The late eighteenth century was a good time for millenarians, religious movements that expected an imminent and total worldly salvation.[16] The rise of science in the seventeenth century had reduced interest in allegorical interpretations of the Bible in favor of more literal approaches. The Book of Revelation, for example, was looked to for a description of real events on earth instead of an allegory of the church. Parallel developments in mathematics, and a general concern for measurement, resulted in an interest in calculation and numbers, and this was applied with renewed vigor to the numerology of the Bible. At the same time, there remained many mystical traditions, with their associated prophets and spiritual thinking, and these were turned to by some as alternative sources of authority in the quest for knowledge about the world.

As the eighteenth century progressed, England became a fertile ground for the spread of the various millenarian movements. A relative lack of censorship, a flourishing newspaper industry (there were fourteen daily newspapers in London alone), and a multitude of printers of pamphlets (of whom Robert was one) meant new ideas could spread rapidly. A heightened interest in curiosities, which supported a number of publications such as the *Gentleman's Magazine* and its imitators, meant unusual new ideas received a ready reception. The Reformation and the English Civil War had already been widely interpreted in millennial terms as part of the triumph of the new Protestant faith, but the political upheavals in

16. For more details of the religious background, see Garrett, *Respectable Folly*, and Garrett, "Swedenborg."

France, culminating in the Revolution of 1789–93, were even more readily interpreted as the tribulations preceding imminent salvation.

In England, Joseph Priestley (1733–1804) represented the rationalist millenarian tradition. He distrusted feelings and mysticism, sought verification of his religion in the fulfilment of biblical prophecy, and was a strong supporter of the French Revolution (attracting the nickname "gunpowder Priestley"). His view of the millennium was one of reason fostered through free inquiry. Meanwhile the Swedish Ambassador to Britain Karl Silfverhjelm (a nephew of Swedenborg) founded a society devoted to the study of hermetic wisdom (a philosophical tradition drawing on ancient sources) and animal magnetism (now known as hypnotism). The distinguished painter Philip de Loutherbourg (1740–1812) dabbled in alchemy—until his wife, in a fit of religious fervor, smashed his crucible—and was an early member of the Theosophical Society. Later, he announced he had the power of healing and prophecy and became a follower of Richard Brothers. Brothers himself thought he was king of the Jews and confidently expected to be the ruler of the New Jerusalem after his predicted fall of all the European monarchies in 1798.

Further south, Avignon was a center of Freemasonry, including its more esoteric and occult offshoots. A wealthy Polish nobleman, Thaddeus Grabianka, helped to found a new Masonic lodge there, devoted to the "Holy Word" revealed by a numerical analysis of the Bible, and later a Société des Illuminés à Avignon, which used the teachings of Swedenborg in a new Masonic rite.

These various movements and groups were interlinked through a widespread interchange of people and ideas. Grabianka's Masonic lodge was composed of noblemen from a number of European countries and received a constant stream of visitors. Silfverhjelm, for example, spent some time with the Theosophical Society, as did two of the followers of Brothers (John Wright and William Brian). Benedict Chastanier, a French surgeon living in London and another early member of the Theosophical Society, had links with members of the Avignon society and had written to tell them of the impending arrival of Wright and Brian. And many visitors to London turned up at the Theosophical Society, with Grabianka, for example, being a regular attendee while in London in 1786.

This was the world that Robert encountered when he began to read the works of Swedenborg in 1782 and sought others to discuss them with. He came from an English, Protestant, evangelical background but entered an international world of diverse ideas competing for attention among intellectuals and others with a thirst for reliable knowledge about the world. Older mystical and alchemical traditions jostled with newer rationalist ideas, and both increasingly incorporated millennial thinking towards the end of the eighteenth century. People mixed across Europe, argued and exchanged ideas, and switched from one movement to another. Robert, for example, personally met with Joseph Priestley, Thaddeus Grabianka, Richard Brothers, and many others.

The first indication of any gathering of those interested in Swedenborg is in a proposal for the publication of Swedenborg's *Spiritual Diary* in 1791,[17] which refers to a society that was "first instituted in the year 1776, for the preservation of Baron Swedenborg's posthumous works" and gives Benedict Chastanier as a contact. There are no details, but the reference fits with an account by Chastanier of his discovery in March 1776 that the author of *Arcana Coelestia*, a work that had intrigued him, was Swedenborg. In response, he said, "I began to do all I could, in order to make these works as publicly known as possible."[18] Chastanier makes no mention of a society, but one of the things he did was to publish two of Swedenborg's works. It may have been that the "society" was merely a group of people willing to finance Chastanier's publishing activity.

Then came Robert's Theosophical Society in 1783, followed in 1789 by the Universal London Society for the Promotion of the New Jerusalem Church (secretary Henry Servanté). A constitution for this society was published in 1790[19] and it also published the *New Jerusalem Magazine* in that year. However, things then start to get rather confusing. Many historians follow Hyde[20] and equate the Universal London Society with the 1776 society in the proposal for the publication of Swedenborg's *Spiritual Diary*, but it is far from clear that this is correct. While the constitution of the Universal London Society has a hint of an earlier existence, it clearly states that it originated in a meeting in August 1789. It also says that there is a need to publish Swedenborg's *Conjugial Love*, which suggests that the society was formed as a response to a controversy over that work earlier in 1789 (see chapter 6). Furthermore, the editors of the *New Jerusalem Magazine* themselves state that "in the year 1783 the first society of the friends

17. Anon., "Proposals."

18. Chastanier, *Word of Advice*, 24.

19. Anon., "Universal London Society."

20. Hyde, "Benedict Chastanier," 188.

to the New Doctrine was formed in London,"[21] which would be very odd for the magazine of a society that was older than that. Similarly, if the two societies were the same, it is strange that the reference in the proposal for the publication of Swedenborg's *Spiritual Diary* doesn't refer to the London Universal Society by name. It seems most likely that the London Universal Society did indeed originate in 1789 and Hyde was wrong to equate it with the possible 1776 society. Robert does not appear to have been associated with the London Universal Society at all and only makes one oblique reference to it in *Rise and Progress* as a small group meeting at Servanté's house that was responsible for publishing the *New Jerusalem Magazine*.[22]

Some of the confusion around all this may have arisen because Chastanier published in 1782 a plan for a universal society (*Plan Général d'une Société Universelle*), aiming to recruit alchemists, cabalists, and occultists to a society of Masons, though it isn't clear if anything came of it. The use of "Société Universelle" in the name is temptingly close to "London Universal Society," which might have led some to seek connections where there are none. Written in French, Chastanier's plan was clearly targeting an elite French-speaking émigré audience. Prospective members had to be distinguished in one of the arts or sciences, be in a position of significant power, or possess great wealth. The Universal London Society, however, despite the similarities in the name, was clearly aimed at a very different, English-speaking audience. According to Schuchard,[23] Chastanier placed an advert in the *Courier de l'Europe: Gazette Anglo-Française* in April 1783 seeking to attract those interested in Swedenborg, but again this would have been aimed at an émigré audience. The source for the existence of the advert appears to be a letter from Carl Nordenskjöld for which two different translations of "dans la gazette" are published. One[24] refers to an advert in "one of the papers" while the other[25] says "in the gazette." Neither specifies the precise publication and there is no sign of the advert in the online edition of the *Courier de l'Europe* so there is some doubt over where the advert appeared, if indeed it did at all.

Meanwhile, Carl Nordenskjöld, who along with his brother Augustus was a leading supporter of Swedenborg in Stockholm, also got confused.

21. Anon., "Annals," 174.
22. Hindmarsh, *Rise and Progress*, 108.
23. Schuchard, "Secret Masonic History," 42.
24. Tafel, *Documents*, 1177.
25. Tafel, "Early History," 543.

In a letter written in 1822[26] he says he was a member while in London of the Philanthropic Society, which in 1783 was very small. "Philanthropic Society" was actually the name of a Swedish society set up in 1786 and, as far as is known, no society of that name existed in London. He then lists a group of people that looks very like the early Theosophical Society of Hindmarsh et al. Nordenskjöld had arrived in England very late in 1783, and so the timing of his remarks fits with the appearance of Robert's advert. Higham[27] considers Robert's account of the origin of the Theosophical Society and Nordenskjöld's letter to be two versions of the same story, both written forty years or more later and mixing up who did what, and this seems a reasonable conclusion.

If all this seems confusing it is hardly surprising, as the sources themselves seem to be confused about various points, all of which makes it difficult to tease out what actually happened. It does, however, emphasize the intellectually chaotic scene in London at the time with various different groups overlapping in ideas and membership. What seems most likely is that Chastanier had a small group around him in the late 1770s that published a couple of Swedenborg's works but did little else. He then revived this group in 1791 for the purposes of trying to publish Swedenborg's *Spiritual Diary*. Meanwhile, Robert formed the Theosophical Society in 1783, which Nordenskjöld visited the following year and described in a letter. The Universal London Society followed in 1789, after the controversy over *Conjugial Love*, but Robert had no association with this group.

Robert's Theosophical Society was a gathering largely composed of the artisan-professional class in London at the time. Robert was a printer and the son of a teacher and preacher, and the first few to join him at the London Coffee House were from similar backgrounds: Peter Provo was an apothecary and later translator of some of Swedenborg's works; William Spence was a doctor and "an extremely honest and benevolent gentleman";[28] William Bonnington was a clock-case maker; Henry Peckitt was a retired apothecary and "a very worthy character" who had been influenced by mystic writers, which left his reading of Swedenborg still "at times tinctured with the coloring derived from his former studies."[29] John Augustus Tulk, a gentleman of independent means who provided some financial firepower

26. Tafel, "Early History," 542.

27. Higham, "London New Church Advertisement," 517.

28. Tafel, *Documents*, 1175.

29. Tafel, *Documents*, 1191.

for the group's publishing ambitions, was the only exception. None of them were part of the subculture of artists, engravers and others interested in all manner of occult things, but they did have an ambitious and internationalist outlook from the start. One of their first actions, in January 1784, was to issue an address, written by Robert, *To the Christian World at Large* to announce their presence to the world—not just London—and the importance of Swedenborg's works.[30] By 1785 they were distributing books to correspondents in various European countries, North and South America, and a number of other places, and by 1787 they were advertising nine of Swedenborg's works as available from Robert.[31]

As they grew in size they began to attract a wider range of people, some of whom brought more foreign influences and had links to various other millennial movements—"dabblers in the occult, alchemy and animal magnetism" as Lineham called them.[32] Some of those in a list of thirty-three "persons of distinguished reputation for talent and merit in their several professions" listed by Robert[33] were: Lt. General Rainsford, later deputy governor of Gibraltar, interested in animal magnetism, alchemy, and astrology and a member of the Société des Illuminés à Avignon; Francois Barthélémon, a French violinist; Benedict Chastanier, whom we have met already, who also had connections to the Avignon society; the painter Philip de Loutherbourg; August and Carl Frederick Nordenskjöld, two Swedish noblemen who had brought some of Swedenborg's works to England; Charles Wadström, a Swede and one of the first agitators against the slave trade; and John Flaxman, a sculptor and friend of William Blake.

The society also attracted some more exotic visitors. Thaddeus Grabianka turned up in 1786, and Robert relates that he gave them to understand that he was in possession of a great secret that would be divulged when the proper time arrived. Some wanted to know what it was, and others considered it a hoax, but it was many months before the proper time came. Eventually it was revealed that the secret was that there were four persons in the Trinity, the fourth being Mary, the mother of Jesus. Robert was scathing:

> If this was the secret purpose or end, for which the Count visited the Society of the New Church in London, he certainly did not succeed in his mission: for not an individual could be found among

30. Hindmarsh, *Rise and Progress*, 24–25.

31. Anon., "Baron Swedenborg."

32. Lineham, "Origins," 112.

33. Hindmarsh, *Rise and Progress*, 23.

> us so weak and so extremely besotted, as to give countenance for a moment to such a visionary, impious, and atrocious creed.[34]

Given the anti-Trinitarian strand of Robert's thinking, the Protestant background of many in the Theosophical Society, and Swedenborgian thinking more generally, the suggestion that Mary should join the Trinity was never going to go down well with the Theosophical Society. Furthermore, there was probably some suspicion of Grabianka as a Catholic and a papist, which a secret about Mary would only enhance. Hyde suggested that the "great secret" was in fact a Masonic one and that Robert had been hoodwinked or had misunderstood,[35] but it is not clear why he thought that. The Avignon society did build a temple in Avignon with four crosses for God, Jesus, the Holy Spirit, and Mary, which would fit with Grabianka's idea of a quaternity.[36] Despite this, and perhaps as a result of the influence of those more sympathetic to his Catholic and Masonic background, Grabianka was elected an honorary member of the Theosophical Society. However, the following year the society voted by twelve to one to refuse admission to William Bousie, who was also associated with the Avignon society.

The suspicion of Catholic influences was reinforced by the tales told by William Bryan and John Wright, who visited Avignon soon afterwards. They had found there a society that believed it had direct communication with heaven, meeting regularly on a mountaintop to converse with an angel. On one occasion, they were introduced to "the actual and personal presence of the Lord," which consisted of a young man in purple garments on a throne. Robert was again scathing and this time made a direct link with Catholicism:

> That any number of Christians, in modern times, should be associated together with principles and practices like these, is indeed an extraordinary phenomenon; and perhaps can only be accounted for by tracing the existence of such a Society to some Jesuitical scheme and contrivance, to extend the dominion of the Romish priesthood over the souls and bodies of men.[37]

34. Hindmarsh, *Rise and Progress*, 45.
35. Hyde, "Benedict Chastanier," 195.
36. Danilewicz, "King of the New," 65.
37. Hindmarsh, *Rise and Progress*, 48–49.

He goes on to relate an anecdote about Bryan with a rather mocking tone (and revealing a wry sense of humor in an otherwise very serious man):

> Of Bryan's enthusiasm the reader may judge from the following anecdote. Walking with him one day in the streets of London, and conversing with him on the subject of some extraordinary powers to which he pretended, beyond those of his fellow-mortals, I desired him to state what these were; when he declared, that he was possessed of a faith sufficient to demolish and remove everything that opposed any obstacle to his wishes. "For example," said he, "were I now disposed to exert my faith, and the power inseparable from it, I could, with a single blast of wind from my mouth, over throw the buildings on either side of the street, and scatter them in all directions." I smiled at the idea, and told him, I hoped he would have the goodness to keep his faith in check for a while, at least until I had an opportunity of securing a safe retreat from the possible danger. He consented to this, and we both walked on, he without blowing up the street by the intensity of his faith, and I without witnessing the dreadful effects of his vaunted power.[38]

Thus Robert encountered an increasingly wide range of people and ideas through the Theosophical Society, but it is less clear how far he was influenced by them. While the quotes above suggest that Robert had no time at all for the views of his more radical contacts, several writers argue that Robert was sufficiently drawn into these circles to feel a need to play down those links when he came to write his *Rise and Progress* in his later years. There are indeed some omissions from *Rise and Progress* that are cited as evidence for this cover-up: for example, he omits some of those listed by Carl Nordenskjöld as active in the Theosophical Society and says little about the ideas the more radical members brought or how they might have influenced the society. He discusses the visit of Grabianka but he doesn't mention the Masonic nature of the Avignon society or that he printed Grabianka's letter to the society (though he did reprint the letter itself in *Rise and Progress*). Another notable omission is a radical pamphlet written by August Nordenskjöld in 1789: *An Address to the True Members of the New Jerusalem Church*. This draws a very strong parallel between alchemy and Swedenborgianism. In alchemy, there is the philosopher's stone, the natural stone that, when discovered, would transform and purify matter. In the works of Swedenborg can be found a spiritual stone, the means whereby

38. Hindmarsh, *Rise and Progress*, 47.

people may be transformed and purified. Nordenskjöld then argues that, just as the New Church has restored spiritual liberty and destroyed the monopoly of the clergy on the meaning of the Bible, so the philosopher's stone will destroy the monopoly of gold and silver in the commercial world. This was a revolutionary political message: alchemy and Swedenborgianism would take away disparities in wealth and inaugurate a new and transformed world. The document concludes by saying,

> PS It is particularly requested, that the contents of this letter be not made public; and that all answers be directed for me at Mr Robert Hindmarsh's, Printer To His Royal Highness the Prince of Wales, No 32 Clerkenwell Close, London.[39]

Robert does not mention this document or that he printed and distributed it.

Schuchard doesn't merely suggest that Robert was influenced by these ideas, but goes much further:

> Hindmarsh deliberately slanted the history to maximize his own role and to serve a counter-revolutionary political agenda. Like Wordsworth, Coleridge, and Southey, Hindmarsh labored to cover up his own early revolutionary leanings and to distance himself and the New Church from charges of subversive "illuminism". By omitting or distorting the dominant role of foreign Freemasons in organizing the New Jerusalem Temple in London, Hindmarsh created a conservative, prudish and inaccurate version of 18th-century Swedenborgianism that fit comfortably into a Victorian milieu.[40]

Thus, she argues, Robert was not merely playing down the occult influences but was drawn fully into the Masonic and radical circles that the likes of Chastanier, Rainsford, and the Nordenskjöld brothers brought to London. She goes on to claim that Robert was a mason and his Theosophical Society was in fact the public arm of the secret Universal London Society. It is a striking hypothesis: had the entirely respectable minister of the New Church of the 1810s and 1820s in fact been a dangerous radical in his youth?

However, if *Rise and Progress* is a cover-up, it isn't a very good one. Robert may have omitted some of those mentioned by Carl Nordenskjöld,

39. Schuchard, "Secret Masonic History," 51.
40. Schuchard, "Secret Masonic History," 40.

but he doesn't seek to hide his association with a wide range of radical characters who would be regarded as dubious at best by the church and the political authorities. He lists many of them and recounts their activities, notably including a lengthy description of the visit of Grabianka, but is generally scathing about their ideas. He describes a meeting with Richard Brothers but dismisses his "folly and madness" and describes Joanna Southcott as "ridiculous." He observes,

> Such are the pretensions, which men in all ages, and sometimes women, have presumptuously made, in order to gain proselytes to their contemptible notions, and thus to counteract and render null those genuine, authentic, and beneficial revelations, which have from time to time been given to mankind.[41]

If Robert was trying to play down his contacts with the radicals in *Rise and Progress* he could clearly have gone much further than he did. He could have said much less, requiring less need of the vigorous dismissal of their ideas. Furthermore, there is evidence from other sources that Robert's views remained consistent and had not changed by the time he wrote his *Rise and Progress*. For example, in 1790 Robert's publication *The New Magazine of Knowledge* carried a number of articles on astrology, spiritualism, and animal magnetism, which are followed by rebuttals by the editors, in one instance scorning "a certain society in France of—what shall we say?—of mystico-cabbalistico-magnetical practitioners."[42] This is a clear reference to the Avignon society. So even back in 1790 Robert is clearly siding against the more esoteric ideas of the time.

Furthermore, some of the claims of the cover-up hypothesis are at best uncertain. As already discussed, there is considerable doubt over whether the Universal London Society even existed in the mid-1780s, let alone that it was a secret society that Robert was actively involved in. Nor does it seem likely that a secret society would publish its own constitution, as the Universal London Society did, or that it would publish a magazine bearing its own name (*The New Jerusalem Magazine* of 1790), one that was in direct competition with a second magazine from its public arm (*The Magazine of Knowledge Concerning Heaven and Hell*) published by Robert in the same year. The so-called secret society was not very secret at all. The editors of *The New Jerusalem Magazine* also stated that the first society in London was

41. Hindmarsh, *Rise and Progress*, 124.

42. Anon., "Remark," 406.

formed in 1783, which would have to have been a calculated falsehood, designed to mislead, if the publishers of the magazine, the Universal London Society, had existed since 1776.

Some of Schuchard's evidence can also be questioned, as there is no record in the United Grand Lodge of England Freemason Membership Registers of Robert having been a Mason. Nor is there any sign of an advert by Chastanier in the online version of the *Courier*. Rix, who follows Schuchard, asserts that Robert makes no mention of Grabianka's visit to London,[43] whereas in fact seven pages of *Rise and Progress* are devoted to it. This all suggests that the evidential basis for the cover-up hypothesis may not be as strong as it looks.

The depth of connection between the early artisan members of the Theosophical Society and the more radical members is also questionable. Carl Nordenskjöld, writing in 1783, is not very complimentary about the former:

> Mr Wright was a clockmaker . . . he was quaker . . . he did not leave his sect. . . . He wished to make me a proselyte, but begged me not to portray his zeal to the members of the society. . . . He took a dislike to me, and endeavoured to injure me. He was the cause that the society was broken up.
>
> Here my kindred in religion are not so affable and hospitable; they reckon much on their simple meal-time food. Some of them have at last invited me for a single time. Herr Spence is the only one who gives me meals, generally once a week. Herr Chastanier means well but, as he is very poor and is not in harmony with his ill-natured wife, I seldom want to go to him. However, they are all in tolerably good circumstances. Herr Pecket is childless and seems to be wealthy. Herr Wright is considered rich, owns several houses in the city, an estate in the country, and has an income of about 1,000 pounds sterling from his Watch Factory. None of them can speak French very well. At first I was much surprised at their rude manners, but now I am used to them. As yet there is not one of them I can thank for any service or courtesy inasmuch as I have given honourable occasion for the little they have shown me. If the English have many advantages, much propriety, and much perfection, they are also puffed up over it, and imagine that none can equal them that none can possess the genius and invention they have. And I now find that the Englishman is a vainglorious creature. When, occasionally, I dispute with my brethren in religion, although I bring forward the best of reasons, they never admit that

43. Rix, "William Blake."

> I am right until I can produce in Swedenborg's works the argument, which refutes them and asserts what I have said. Moreover, they are all extremely uninformed in the new Doctrine.[44]

Henry Servanté too did not find everyone agreeable. Writing to James Glen in 1806[45] he says he never considered William Spence a true recipient, as he remained opposed to separation and strongly asserted that only those ordained by a Bishop were qualified or authorized to preach the doctrines of Swedenborg. These letters do not describe a society where the radical and conservative members all coexisted happily. They rather suggest two groups with very different backgrounds—conservative English Nonconformists and Lineham's foreign "dabblers in the occult, alchemy and animal magnetism"—united by a common interest in Swedenborg but sitting rather uneasily alongside each other. Robert's background was very much in the first group and his alignment with them was confirmed when he joined with others in that group to form the separate New Church (see chapter 4).

Perhaps most telling, Schuchard's hypothesis would require Robert to change suddenly from a critical Nonconformist, steeped in his Methodist background, to one of Lineham's dabblers and then equally suddenly back again as he pursued a very conservative political and ecclesiastical agenda in the infant New Jerusalem Church a few years later (see chapter 8). In contrast, *Rise and Progress* has a psychological coherence and consistency that fits with Robert's writings in the 1790s and other times, and the criticism of the wilder characters and ideas Robert encountered read true to his essential character. If Robert played down the extent and influence of Lineham's dabblers, it is more likely because they played a much smaller role in the development of the New Jerusalem Church once it had separated itself as a distinct organization. While some of the foreigners (Chastanier, Nordenskjöld, Servanté, and Wadström) were present at the first conference of the New Church in 1789 and on the committee that signed its minutes, none of them were part of the group that began the New Church as a separate organization or the group that ordained its first ministers (contrary to Schuchard's assertion that they played a dominant role). They were perhaps more interested in the ideas than the institution, while for Robert the institution was central.

Robert's account of the visit of Grabianka is instructive in teasing out Robert's relationship with the radicals. He clearly enjoyed the visit of this

44. Nordenskjöld, "CF Nordenskjöld."

45. Servanté, "Epistolary Correspondence III," 419.

exotic, charismatic foreigner, saying that the count was always interesting and animated and everyone was delighted by his company. However, while Grabianka might have been fun to be with, this did not make his ideas any more agreeable, and Robert is very clear about his contempt for them. In the context of everything else we know, a plausible reading of this account is that Robert was fascinated by the more exotic people and ideas he encountered but felt no pull towards them and, in the end, he had little time for them.

3

Printer and Translator

ROBERT COMPLETED HIS APPRENTICESHIP around 1780 and by 1782, when he began looking for others with an interest in Swedenborg, he had his own printing business in London at 3 Bakers Court, Holborn, just off the present A40 road near to Chancery Lane underground station (though the court has long since been demolished). By 1783 he had moved half a mile or so to 32 Clerkenwell Close, presumably to larger and better premises, and this was to be his home and place of work for the next eleven years. Again the building has long since been demolished, with the present one with that address dating from 1889.

Clerkenwell was initially a small village just to the north of the City of London, but by the late seventeenth century it was growing rapidly, particularly following the devastation in London caused by the great fire of 1666. The housing was quite varied, with rents in 1677 varying from £2 to £40 per year, reflecting the significant proportion of housing for the gentry and more prosperous tradesmen. By 1708 there were 1,146 houses in the parish, growing to 1,900 by 1732 and 4,995 by 1821. Horwood's *Plan of London* shows that Clerkenwell was on the edge of the London conurbation in the 1790s, with open fields to the north.[1]

Until the dissolution of the monasteries under Henry VIII, the village had included a Benedictine nunnery, founded in the twelfth century, and Clerkenwell Close was originally part of the area enclosed by the boundary

1. Horwood, *Plan*.

wall of the nunnery.[2] Of 134 "merchants, manufacturers and principal tradesmen" in Clerkenwell in 1794, the most common (25 percent of the total) were watchmakers, clockmakers, and related trades, followed by goldsmiths and/or silversmiths (6 percent). There were two printers, including Robert, one printer-ink maker, and three engravers. Sixteen traders are listed in Clerkenwell Close (out of thirty-five numbered houses on Horwood's Plan) with trades including silversmith, watchmaker, enameler, engraver, and portrait painter.[3] This was the place where Robert lived: a mixture of gentry and skilled workers living in nice, brick-built houses set in cobbled streets with pavements and a central drain.

In 1787, much to his own delight, Robert was appointed Printer Extraordinaire to the Prince of Wales, though what he may have printed for the prince is not known. In 1794 he became a Freeman of the City of London and a member of the Stationers' Company by redemption (i.e., he paid for it rather than it being as the result of an apprenticeship), which is slightly odd as he had been an apprentice printer, so maybe he never formally completed the apprenticeship. During this time all three of his sons are listed as his apprentices, but only Henry went on to become a Freeman of the City of London (by servitude, which is similarly odd as he only ever appears in records as a solicitor; perhaps he was a printer for a short time first). Only one other apprentice is listed—a Michael Allen of Paternoster Row who was bound for seven years from October 6, 1795. Clerkenwell Close in turn ceased to serve Robert's needs, and by 1794 he had built a new house and printing works at 15 Old Bailey, and he remained there until at least 1797.

In the late eighteenth century, printing was still essentially the same as the process that had been introduced to Europe by Gutenberg around 1450. The technology had improved a little but the design of the press and the basic processes were largely unchanged. The first step was the arrangement of the type, the highly skilled craft of the compositor. The moveable type (pieces of cast metal with a letter or other symbol in relief) were arranged in a tray to create a page of text, with the skill being in arranging the letters, words, and spaces in such a way as to create, at speed, a neat and readable page of text (without, of course, any of the automation of a modern word processor). The arranged text was then transferred to a larger sliding tray on the press itself, which might have several pages of text if the pages of the

2. Pinks, *History of Clerkenwell*, 90.

3. Wakefield, *Wakefield's Merchant*, title page.

finished book were smaller than the sheets of paper in the press. The ink was then placed on two leather balls, which were worked together to make the ink even and then pressed onto the type to transfer the ink to the type. The paper was placed on a hinged frame attached to the sliding tray containing the type and folded down on top of the type. The whole assembly was slid under the center of the press where a handle was pulled, which, through the action of a screw, pressed the paper down onto the type. The tray was then slid out again for the now printed paper to be removed and the whole process repeated. A press working at full speed could print 250 sheets of paper on one side in an hour, or about one every fifteen seconds.[4]

According to the *English Short Title Catalogue* at the British Library, which lists nearly half a million titles published before 1800, Robert was the printer of 146 works. Around two thirds of these are either by Swedenborg or related to Swedenborg or the New Church, so it is clear that a major part of the output of the press was aimed at furthering the Swedenborgian cause. The rest are diverse and include a Hebrew grammar, various scientific works, books of poems, and a compendium of the laws of Montserrat. Many of the books were also sold by Robert, and an advertisement with the minutes of a conference of the New Church in 1789 gives a sense of the scale of activity.[5]

List of Books Printed and Sold By R Hindmarsh, Printer To His Royal Highness The Prince of Wales, No 32 Clerkenwell-Close, London	*£*	*s*	*d*
True Christian Religion, or the Universal Theology of the New Church	0	15	0
A Treatise on the Nature of Influx, or of the Communication between Soul and Body	0	1	6
Treatise concerning Heaven and Hell	0	4	0
Of the New Jerusalem and it's Heavenly Doctrine	0	4	0
The Doctrine of the New Jerusalem concerning the Lord	0	2	0
The Doctrine of the New Jerusalem concerning the Sacred Scripture	0	2	0
The Doctrine of Life for the New Jerusalem	0	1	6
Of the Earths in the Universe	0	2	6

4. Moxon, *Mechanik Exercises*, 427.
5. Anon., *Minutes of the First*, 43.

The Psalms of David, with a Summary Exposition of the Internal Sense	0	3	0
Of the White Horse mentioned in the Revelation, Chapter XIX with curious Remarks on the Souls of Beasts, and the Life of Vegetables	0	1	0
An Eulogium delivered on the Death of the Author, &c	0	0	6
A Summary View of the principal Doctrines contained in the Writings of Emanuel Swedenborg	0	1	6
A Treatise concerning the Last Judgment, and the Destruction of Babylon, which took place in the Spiritual World in the Year 1757	0	2	6
Angelic Wisdom concerning Divine Love and Divine Wisdom	0	6	0
The Liturgy of the New Church, signified by the New Jerusalem in the Revelation; including the Forms for the Administration of Baptism and the Holy Supper	0	1	0
Nine Queries concerning the Trinity, &c with their Answers	0	0	3
A Short Account of the Hon E Swedenborg, and his Theological Writings	0	0	6
Extracts from the Manuscripts of Emanuel Swedenborg	0	0	2

Four of the books in this list (*Treatise on the Nature of Influx*, *Of the White Horse*, *Treatise Concerning the Last Judgement*, and *Nine Queries Concerning the Trinity*) had been translated by Robert himself. Given that the earnings of a general laborer were about two shillings a day, these books were clearly only affordable by the wealthier citizens of London at the time.

A list of all the editions of Swedenborg's works published before the foundation of the Swedenborg Society in 1825, drawn up by Robert and printed in *Rise and Progress*, lists nine that were translated by Robert from the original Latin, seven of which he printed at his own expense. A further three works were printed in Latin at his own expense. Clearly he spent a considerable amount of time on translation and provided significant financial backing to make those translations available to the public. Nothing is known directly about Robert's printing business apart from its location—there are no details of turnover, output, staff employed, and so on. However, it is possible to draw some tentative conclusions from the details of works that it is known he printed. For fifty-nine of the books in the *English Short Title Catalogue*, the number of pages, the size of the final book (which determines the number of sheets of paper required, as four or eight pages were usually printed on one sheet), and the price at which it was sold are available, and this, along with some reasonable estimates, allows some calculations to be made.

The 146 works in the catalog would have required around 1.7 million sheets of paper and around five years of press operation to complete, and would have yielded an income in the region of £13,000. Given that Robert's press was in operation for about fourteen years, these are almost certainly underestimates, and indeed it is known that he printed many pamphlets that did not make their way into the *English Short Title Catalogue.* If the 146 works in the catalog were about half of the total output, this gives a total income of £26,000.[6] Assuming a margin of 30 percent (it was probably reasonably high as he sold many of the books himself as well as printing them so would accrue the seller's profit as well), this gives Robert an income of about £550 per year. This is comparable with eminent clergy or people who were living off private income and was more than the income of typical lawyers, engineers, or shopkeepers.[7] This puts Robert in a very comfortable position and explains how he was able to finance the publication of books and magazines, contribute significantly to the building of chapels, and build himself a new house and print works at Old Bailey.

It would also have enabled him to provide a comfortable life for his family. He had married Sarah Paramor in 1782 and he had five children with her. Henry, born in 1783, became an apprentice printer under his father but for most of his life was a solicitor in London. Elizabeth, born in 1785, married Thomas Hodson, who may have been related to other Hodsons who appear in early New Church records. Charles, born in 1788, was also a solicitor but died of tuberculosis at the age of just 44. His obituary remarks that he was never a member of the New Church but adhered to its doctrines.[8] Of Jane Hindmarsh, born 1789, nothing is known save that she married a man called Heap. Similarly, little is known of George, born in 1790, except that he lived in Walworth, Surrey, and it may be that

6. The assumptions used for the printing calculation were two hundred sheets per hour operating for six hours per day (Moxon says twelve hours, but time would be needed for changing type trays, maintenance, etc.) and three hundred days per year, with a print run of five hundred for each book (this was the most common print run of one of the largest London printers in the eighteenth century; see Hernlund, "William Strahan's Ledgers") and 75 percent of each run actually sold. Putting a wide margin of error on each of these assumptions still yields an income for Robert of £370 to £900 per year.

7. Lindert and Williamson, "Revising England's Social Tables," 393.

8. Hindmarsh, "Obituary [of Charles Hindmarsh]."

Robert resided with him there for a while in the late 1790s. Remarkably, all five children survived into adulthood at a time when parents could expect around one third of their children to die before the age of five. The lifestyle Robert was able to afford would have helped, but mortality was still high even among the wealthy, and so he and his wife Sarah were very fortunate parents.

4

A New Church

INITIALLY, THERE WAS NO attempt among Robert's gathering of the readers of Swedenborg's works to create a separate church. In the January 1784 address "To the Christian World at Large," they claimed they "wish[ed] nothing more than to renounce every appearance of a sectarian spirit."[1] Gradually, however, a number of factors propelled some of Robert's society towards a more sectarian, separatist view.

Many of them, like Robert, came from a Nonconformist background and so were used to gathering for services around a set of beliefs rather than an institution, and to the idea that they might build their own chapels. Many were also ex-Methodists, drawn to Swedenborg at a time when Wesley was preventing Methodism from seceding from the Anglican Church (and some, such as Isaac Hawkins, had been expelled from Methodism for their beliefs). As Protestants they already saw the Bible as a God-given source of authority, and now they took a high view of the authority of Swedenborg's works as also having a heavenly origin (as Robert had declared about his own second encounter with them). This sharpened their sense of difference from what they termed "the old church" and tended to lead to a rejection of those who did not agree with their views.

Meanwhile the foreign members of the society, while in some ways sitting uneasily alongside the English Protestants, brought a radicalism to their thinking. Many were strongly influenced by the revolutionary times

1. Hindmarsh, *Rise and Progress*, 24–25.

in France, and this helped to heighten an apocalyptic atmosphere. Francis Dobbs visited the society in 1786 and

> met nearly thirty persons, all of whom believed they had reasons out of the common order of things to think that these times could produce mighty changes, that would end in the establishment of human happiness.[2]

As the group grew in size and self-confidence, these forces began to do their work but, as separation was a far from unanimous view, the New Church began in schism. Robert was a "leading spirit"[3] and a "strenuous supporter"[4] of the separatists, and Odhner describes his leadership in typical adulatory terms:

> Led by the ever resolute and fearless Robert Hindmarsh, some of the members of the society resolved to lay before their brethren a proposal to open a place for the distinctive public worship of the Lord Jesus Christ.[5]

Robert had a theological rationale for separation, which went back to one of his reasons for being attracted to Swedenborg: the old church was entirely pervaded by the idea of a Trinity of gods, which subverted its very foundations; therefore there was a clear need for a new church where the Lord Jesus Christ as the supreme and only God could be worshiped. He also justified the move in practical terms, a desire to see the followers of Swedenborg grow more rapidly. In this he was reflecting his Methodist background where Wesley always looked to the primacy of mission. Wesley was a man of action whose purpose was to help people find their way to salvation, and he would do what was necessary to achieve that, even if it didn't go down well with the established church. Robert, similarly, was driven by a desire to make more converts to the Swedenborgian cause:

> It had been found, after a trial of several years, that the progress of the Church, in procuring actual recipients of the doctrines, by merely publishing the works, and by holding meetings for reading and conversation, was comparatively very partial in its extent. And it was thought, that the promise and hope of increase to the Church attached more to the hearing of the Word preached, than

2. Dobbs, *Concise View*, 250.
3. Abbott, "Establishment," 150.
4. Editors, "Rev Robert Hindmarsh," 414.
5. Odhner, *Robert Hindmarsh*, 17.

> to the reading of comment upon it, or to any private explanations that may be given of it, however edifying they may be to those who have already embraced the new doctrines.[6]

A proposal to open a place of worship was put to the society at a meeting on April 19, 1787 but was rejected by a small majority. Despite this Robert and some others decided to go ahead anyway, meeting separately for the first time on May 7. The minutes list thirteen names including the president (Thomas Wright), secretary (Robert Hindmarsh) and treasurer (Henry Pickett) of the former society along with James Hindmarsh, Isaac Hawkins (the friend of James we met earlier) and eight others. In effect, the thirteen created a new society with the same name as the old one, but they carried on as if nothing had happened. The officers refused to give up the lease on the room in the Middle Temple, so they even retained the same meeting place. Their first act, in a new minute book, was to record the circumstances of this decision:

> A misunderstanding having arisen among the members of the Society for Promoting the Heavenly Doctrines of the New Jerusalem Church, held in the Middle Temple, concerning the original design for which they met; and a majority of the members present at a meeting held on Thursday the 19th of April 1787 having determined to change the mode of conducting the Society, the following persons, whose names are hereunto subscribed, members of the said society, fully sensible of the great utility which has attended their meetings, when conducted on the former plan, agree, by the Divine mercy of the Lord, to form themselves into a new Society under the same name as that above mentioned, and for the same purposes as heretofore, to be continued and held at the same time and place as before.[7]

This resolution is surprising as it claims that it was the majority that had tried to "change the mode of conducting the Society," implying that this new, separatist group was merely trying to keep the aim of separation against a majority who wished to change to being non-separatist. This is something of a turnaround from their initial declaration of "renouncing a sectarian spirit."[8] Robert claims that the society "unanimously Resolved,

6. Hindmarsh, *Rise and Progress*, 53.

7. Anon., "Great East Cheap Minute."

8. An alternative explanation is that this transcript of the minute book (the original does not survive) mistakenly omitted the word "not" and so inadvertently changed the meaning.

that, on the first opportunity that might offer, a suitable chapel, situate in some convenient part of the town, should be engaged for the use of the Society,"[9] but the minute book does not record this.

It is notable that the list of thirteen people present does not include any of the foreign or radical members of Robert's society. However, at a second meeting on May 7, they agreed to admit fifteen people who had been honorary members of the previous society, including Mr. Nordenskjöld (probably August), Count Grabianka, Marquis de Thome and Mr. Gosse. This suggests they wished to retain their links with the foreign members, though it is notable that none of the foreign members (and indeed only three out of the fifteen) attended any of the Thursday business meetings. This perhaps reflects a greater interest among the foreigners in the ideas of Swedenborgianism rather than the institutional form it took (though they may have attended worship on Sundays). The new society went on to agree a set of rules on July 2 that included the requirement that members must be elected by a unanimous vote of existing members, enhancing their sense of a separate group taking forward the Swedenborgian cause.

What Robert describes as a "select meeting . . . of those persons most anxious to bring forward the New Church" met on July 29, 1787 at Thomas Wright's house (the man Carl Nordenskjöld considered responsible for the breakup in the society).[10] Here they heard a paper read by James Glen, who had recently returned from Demerara in South America, where there had been an attempt to found a Swedenborgian colony, and who was infused with a sense of the millenarian significance of Swedenborgianism. Seven of the thirteen present (including James Glen, John Augustus Tulk, and two women, Margaret Parker and Jane Grant) were not members of the new society at the time, though all except the two women were subsequently admitted. The other members may not even have known what was happening. It is worth noting the principles of the New Church included in James Glen's paper, as it provides a neat summary of the group's thinking at the time:[11]

Four Principles of the Doctrine of Influx

1 There are two distinct Worlds, the Spiritual and the Natural.

2 The Spiritual World produces the Natural World by Influx.

9. Hindmarsh, *Rise and Progress*, 56.

10. Tafel, "Early History," 544.

11. Hindmarsh, *Rise and Progress*, 57.

3 In consequence of this Influx, every Object in Nature corresponds with its Spiritual cause.

4 This Correspondence, by means of Influx, is essential to the Existence of both Worlds.

Four Theological Parallels

1 God Omnipotent in his Divine Humanity, in the year 1757, began and accomplished a Last Judgment in the Spiritual World, and thereby formed New Heavens.

2 From these New Heavens a New Church will descend, must descend, on this earth, according to the eternal and immutable Laws of Influx.

3 This New Church will be an exact Corresponding Representation of the New Heavens.

4 This Correspondence, by Influx, between the New Heavens and the New Church, is essential to the Existence of both.

Observations Added

1 The Truths of the New Church are *alone* contained in the Word, and the Theological Writings of Emanuel Swedenborg.

2 The Doctrine of Correspondence, being the Knowledge of the Order of Influx, as proceeding from the Divine Humanity, is essential to the Understanding of the Word.

3 The earnest and hearty Rejection of the Doctrines and Forms of the Old Church, must precede the full Reception of the Influx of Wisdom and Love from the Divine Humanity, through the New Heavens, into the New Church.

4 The full Reception of the glorious Truths of the New Church, as revealed by Swedenborg, is essential to constitute a Member of the New Church on earth, and thereby to admit him into an immediate Conjunction with the Lord, and Consociation with the Angels of the New Heavens.

5 Introduction into the New Church is solely through the Spiritual Correspondent, Baptism, performed in that Church.

6 Conjunction with the Lord, and Consociation with the Angels of the New Heavens, are effected by the Holy Supper taken in the New Church, according to Heavenly and Divine Correspondences.

The "Observations Added" are notable for indicating that the works of Swedenborg are an equal source of truth to the Bible, and that full reception of Swedenborg's works is essential to being a member of the New Church. In other words, the separatists had moved on from being "receivers" of Swedenborg's ideas, who discussed and explored them in the context of the old church, to being "believers" who felt compelled to institutionalize their new beliefs. They also agreed that entry to the New Church is through baptism, something that needed to happen. Having unanimously agreed on this statement, the meeting decided to put their intention into effect two days later on the following Tuesday.

That day the thirteen, with the addition of James Hindmarsh and two others, met and chose James by lot to officiate as priest. Eleven of those present, who were not to be baptized, took Communion, and then Robert Hindmarsh was called and asked if he wished to be baptized into the New Heaven and the New Church. He answered in the affirmative and was baptized by his father. Four others were then called together and likewise baptized. It is not at all clear why the five baptized did not take Communion, nor why James Hindmarsh was not baptized (leading to the curious situation whereby the five were baptized into membership by someone who was not himself a baptized member), nor why there were no more baptisms until nearly a year later. Notwithstanding this rather puzzling beginning, Robert described it as "the commencement of the New Church in its External and Visible Form, in the city of London."[12]

Robert was very much on the side of the separatists as secretary of the new society and the first to put himself forward for baptism, but as the split in the Theosophical Society implies, his view was far from being a consensus in the wider Swedenborgian movement. John Clowes was a leading advocate of Swedenborg's works but from within his role as an Anglican rector in Manchester. He was from a wealthy, high church background, with a reputation for piety and a certain otherworldliness, but was a supporter of Sunday schools and limitations on the exploitation of children in factories. He first encountered Swedenborg's works in 1773 and from 1779 began to incorporate the ideas into his preaching and writing. A group of friends came together to support his efforts to publish more of Swedenborg's works, and he held regular meetings in his home (largely composed of workers and artisans) to read and discuss Swedenborg. In 1783 a sermon that seemed to depart from a traditional view of the Trinity sparked opposition to Clowes, inflamed by his supposed fomenting of working-class identity through the meetings he held. There were pamphlets and counter-pamphlets until eventually the bishop of Chester was forced to intervene. Clowes was fortunate in that the bishop himself was less than rigorously

12. Hindmarsh, *Rise and Progress*, 58.

orthodox, did not respect the chief opponent of Clowes, and was known to be tolerant of high- and low-church extremes.

The two clergymen met and Clowes was interrogated. He said he fully accepted the Thirty-Nine Articles of the Anglican faith and believed they could be reconciled with a Swedenborgian position, but it seems the two men came away with different views of what they had agreed. Clowes thought he had license to carry on, though perhaps a little more carefully, while the bishop thought he had forbidden all intrusions of Swedenborgianism. However, the bishop was not inclined to force out Clowes, and so he remained in his position until he died in 1831.

Thus Clowes had direct experience of a dominant, established church feeling strong enough to tolerate divergence of views. He was tolerated, at least in part, because he had no wish to break down that establishment. In this he was like Swedenborg himself, who, coming from the established Lutheran Church of Sweden, never imagined the possibility of separation. This was very different to the experience of the Dissenters, who gathered around a set of ideas and practices and needed to maintain their purity in order to define themselves against the established church. Isaac Hawkins was, after all, expelled by the Methodists for similar behavior to Clowes among the Methodists. Clowes's view was that the church was the universal body of believers throughout the world, which could not be identified with a particular group of believers. The new church therefore had to grow within the old one as a renewal of it and not as a separate organization alongside it. Swedenborg's writings were an aid to individual regeneration, and thus the new church would be born in the lives of individuals. For Clowes, bringing the internal church, as it existed in the hearts of believers, in line with the external church meant waiting for the external church to grow to maturity. For Robert and the separatists there was no time to wait, and a new external church had to be created to bring the internal and external churches into line.[13] Despite Clowes's stance, many of his own followers decided to separate and form their own society in Salford.

Robert records that the rejection of the idea of a new organization in 1787 was on the grounds that it was too bold a venture for a group of people lacking both numbers and property, but the group was probably also influenced by views similar to those of Clowes, who remained strongly opposed to separation. Clowes even came to London around November 1787 to try to dissuade the society from separating, and there was an exchange of

13. Ward, "Swedenborgianism," 305.

correspondence culminating in a printed document entitled "Reasons for Separating from the Old Church"[14] in late 1788. It was written and printed by Robert and signed by seventy-seven people (including twenty-three women, not normally signatories to documents of the society), though only thirty-six had been baptized in the New Church at the time. The signatories included many prominent Swedenborgians, but only Servanté, Chastanier, and Wadström from the more radical foreigners, perhaps, as suggested earlier, reflecting their greater interest in the ideas of Swedenborg rather than the institutional form. Only forty-three of the names appear in the Great Eastcheap minute book, showing a wider group involved with the nascent church than took part in its formal business.

Those non-separatist views did not go away, lingering long after the events of 1787. Over time, John Clowes and Robert Hindmarsh became symbolic of this divide and were each held up as representatives of their different views. Barrett, writing over sixty years later, says sectarianism had been the bane of the Christian church and goes on to draw a contrast between Clowes and Hindmarsh:

> Two individuals have, in a pre-eminent degree, left their impress upon the Church of the New Jerusalem; one upon the invisible and real, the other, upon the visible and nominal, New Church. Both were men of eminent ability; but one was remarkable for his humility, charity, catholicity and piety, while in the other these graces were not particularly conspicuous. Both were sincere receivers and zealous advocates of the doctrines of the New Church; but while one seemed to receive them into his heart and to experience their renewing power, the other seemed to receive them only into his head—his intellect. Both claimed to be New-Churchmen; but one saw the New Church wherever he saw a humble and devoted follower of the Lord Jesus Christ, whatever his creed or outward church relations, while the other saw it only among those who openly professed the doctrines taught by Swedenborg, and formally separated themselves from all other Christians.[15]

Abbott drew a similar contrast but was more generous towards Robert:

> Their speech was powerful, but not of the same tone; one soft and persuasive, the other strong and trenchant. Their pens were subtle, but not wielded with the same stroke; one piercing the heart of error, the other cleaving its front. The influence of one was

14. Reprinted in Hindmarsh, *Rise and Progress*, 75–78.

15. Barrett, *Catholicity*, 264.

> through the will to the understanding; of the other, through the understanding to the will. Like two neighbouring stars, of similar brilliance, but in which the spectrum might indicate different lines in the composition of the light. Their common joy was "the peace of Jerusalem." Both were men of marked humility. No sectarian or party strife is recorded of their lives.[16]

Robinson also lamented the existence of sectarianism and sought to undermine the whole basis of the New Church:

> They agreed that Introduction into the New Church is *solely* by "Baptism in that Church!" Yet they met together, and eleven of them partook of the Holy Supper together, *none of whom had been baptized into the faith of the New Church*; and they called this act the "commencement of the New Church in its external and visible form!" How could these men do this "most holy" act of worship *in* the New Church, when, according to their own decision, *none of them were in* that Church, at the time? How could their officiating minister perform this "Holy Rite" in that Church, when he himself was not in? How could he baptize five individuals on that occasion with a baptism he himself was not baptized with? . . . Is it not quite clear, that this New Jerusalem Church . . . is altogether spurious in its origins and claims, as an Authoritative Institution? It is not the Church of our Lord; but the Church of James Hindmarsh, Robert Hindmarsh, Samuel Smith, and Company![17]

It is perhaps no coincidence that both Barrett (1863) and Robinson (1864) published shortly after the publication of Robert's *Rise and Progress* in 1861, and they show how different views of the issue of separation determined his posthumous reputation. A review of Robinson's *Remembrancer and Recorder* identifies this key issue and consigns it to history:

> The question raised is that of separation, or non-separation, from the external forms and worship of the Old Church (called by ES the Reformed Church). To all separatists the difficulty has been solved, and is no longer a matter of doubt. Those who are interested in it, as a question, must be individuals who have not yet carried their convictions so far as to leave the Old Church. . . . What can be the advantage of now resuscitating the adverse idea, is beyond our apprehension. The non-separatists (whose cause is advocated by the work under notice) cannot expect that the establishment of the

16. Abbott, "Establishment," 155.

17. Robinson, *Remembrancer and Recorder*, 92.

> external New Church will be ever again absorbed in the forms and ceremonies of the Old. However doubtful or anomalous the origin of the present priesthood or ministry of the New Church may have been; custom is so powerful that it will and does answer for law. That authority which may be doubtful in its first efforts gains as it proceeds, and the Conference ministry will still flourish when the *Remembrancer* is consigned to deserved oblivion.[18]

Essentially the reviewer takes a pragmatic view: things might have been a bit messy at the start (and what can you expect when trying to set up a radically new organization from scratch?), but once you are up and running there isn't much point in raking over how it happened. This was the very pragmatism displayed by Robert, reflecting his Methodist background and his desire to get the New Church started.

The review also mentions that Robert had, at the 1833 conference in Bath, told "a gentleman now residing there" that Clowes had admitted to him that he had made a mistake in not separating from the old church. This is probably a reference to a handwritten note by John Wickham Barnes in a copy of Robinson's *Remembrancer and Recorder* in the Swedenborg Society Library. Barnes recalls Robert staying with him for the duration of the conference and telling him that, in his last conversation with John Clowes, Clowes had said, "Friend Hindmarsh, I now see clearly that if I had come forth as you and many hundreds have done and left the Old Church, I could have done twenty times the good I have done."[19] It is hearsay, but Robert knew Clowes from the latter's visit to London in 1787 and, when he moved to Salford, his home was less than a mile from Clowes's church, and so it is highly likely that they would have met and conversed on the progress of the New Church. Clowes had defended his non-separatist view in 1818[20] on the grounds that the New Church lacked the strength to separate. However, Robert claimed in 1817 that Clowes was warming to the idea of separation: he [Clowes] had seen a pamphlet repeating his arguments against separation and had the entire print run bought up and destroyed. "Yet, if the question happens to be touched upon in company he adheres to his old opinion."[21] For Clowes, who had spent much of his life waiting for the new doctrines to take hold and transform the old church, it wouldn't be

18. Anon., "Review: A Remembrancer," 128–29.
19. Wainscot, "Interesting Historical Document," 463.
20. Clowes, *Letter*.
21. Hindmarsh, "Letter of Rev," 103.

surprising if, towards the end of life, seeing no sign of such a transformation, he began to wonder if he had been wrong to wait.

The apogee of the separatist view was reached in Odhner's biography, where Robert is an almost godlike figure who can do no wrong. The result is that much of our knowledge of Robert Hindmarsh comes from a somewhat self-serving autobiographical work alongside other authors who either exalt or demonize him depending on where they sit on the separatist divide. But, if the issue of separation divided the early Swedenborgians, that was nothing compared to the controversy surrounding Robert and the first ordinations.

5

Lottery Tickets

ROBERT AND HIS CO-SEPARATISTS in their new society held weekly meetings on Sundays at the Middle Temple until November 5, 1787, when they were ejected for reasons that are not clear. They then met in members' houses until a chapel in Maidenhead Court, Great Eastcheap,[1] became available at £30 per year. The repurposed chapel opened on January 27, 1788 and had the words "Now it is Allowable" over the entrance. This was a quote from Swedenborg's *True Christian Religion*: "Now it is allowable to enter intellectually into the Mysteries of Faith."[2] James Hindmarsh, Robert's father, was appointed the first minister. The non-separatist group continued to meet for a while, but eventually faded and ceased to meet altogether.

The new congregation held services each Sunday in the morning and afternoon; in the evening there was a meeting for conversation and discussion of Swedenborg's works in which Robert

> took the lead, not only as reader, but also, because, from the assiduity with which he had pursued the study of the heavenly doctrines, he was well,—I may say, the best qualified, to answer both the inquiries of serious minds, and the objections of gainsayers, that might be made at these meetings. Moreover, he had the happy talent of always retaining a composure of mind, and of being able to give an answer to whatever was proposed, or inquired of him, immediately, without any hesitation.

1. In the old City of London between St. Paul's Cathedral and the Tower of London.
2. Swedenborg, *True Christian Religion*, 474.

> At that period, he might be said to be the life and soul of the Society.[3]

While the congregation had the services of James Hindmarsh as a minister, they soon began to consider the establishment of a regular ministry through ordination. They debated in many meetings (though not ones recorded in the official minute book) where such ordination might come from and whether there was any necessity of continuity with ordination in the old church. Eventually, according to Robert, they concluded that a new church could not be subject to the authority of the old church, and that the injunction in Revelation "behold I make all things new" (21:5) applied to the institutions and ordinances of the New Church as much as its doctrines. Hence, ordination had to commence within the New Church from the authority of the immediate presence of the Lord and not from any priesthood of the old church. This, they considered, was the situation faced by the early Christian church, which of necessity had to commence ordination from within itself.[4] Furthermore, no one individual had any right or authority to commence that ordination, and so it was agreed that twelve persons should be selected to represent the whole body of the New Church and this should be done by lot as the only means they had of determining the divine will. Once again they appealed to the early church, who used the lot to determine who should take the place of Judas among the twelve disciples. Some support for this approach could be found in the works of Swedenborg where he refers to a case of the drawing of lots, after which an angel says, "Do not suppose that this Lot came to Hand by mere Chance, but know that it is by Divine Direction."[5]

On Sunday, May 10, 1788, the society (on a proposal by Robert, seconded by his father James) agreed to change its name from "The Society for Promoting the Heavenly Doctrines of the New Jerusalem Church" to "The New Church signified by the New Jerusalem in the Revelation." This was a subtle shift of emphasis from the idea of promoting particular doctrines to an institution rooted in the book of Revelation, from a group of readers to a millennial church. The following Sunday, James Hindmarsh and Samuel Smith baptized each other, the first two baptisms since Robert and the four others a year earlier, in preparation for the first ordinations. Then, on Sunday June 1, 1788, twelve members (out of sixteen present) were chosen by

3. Editors, "Rev Robert Hindmarsh," 415.
4. Hindmarsh, *Rise and Progress*, 68.
5. Swedenborg, *True Christian Religion*, 609.

lot to ordain James Hindmarsh and Samuel Smith. Robert described what happened:

> Being Secretary to the Society, when it was determined, that twelve men should be selected by Lot from the body of the Church, to lay their hands on the heads of persons to be ordained, it was my office to prepare the tickets. I accordingly made sixteen tickets, answering to the number of male persons present, members of the Church, and marked twelve of them with a cross. Being desirous, for my own private satisfaction, to ascertain which of the twelve to be selected by Lot, it might please the Lord to appoint to read or perform the ceremony, I wrote, unknown to the rest of the Society, upon one of the twelve tickets, thus marked with a cross, the word ORDAIN. I then put the sixteen tickets into a receiver, when a prayer went up from my heart, that the Lord would shew whom he had chosen for the office of Ordination. The members being properly arranged, I went round them all; and each one took a ticket out of the receiver, leaving me the last ticket, on which was written, as before stated, the word ORDAIN. Still the other members of the Society were not aware of what I had done; and when the twelve were separated from the rest, after consulting together a few moments, they unanimously requested, that I would read and perform the ceremony of Ordination. Whereupon James Hindmarsh was first ordained by me, and immediately afterwards Samuel Smith.[6]

As with the issue of separation, Robert and the Eastcheap congregation took the pragmatic approach, doing what they deemed necessary to move the society forward in the direction they wanted, once again following the example of John Wesley. Just four years earlier Wesley and two others had ordained two preachers to minister among American Methodists when the bishop of London had refused to do so, seeing it as a pragmatic response to a desperate need.[7] However, this simple act of selecting twelve representatives, laying hands on two men, and proclaiming them ordained, an act in which Robert was a leading player, unleashed a controversy that was at least as deep and fervent as that over separation and rumbled on for decades. The minutes of various conferences of the New Church held in the following years show signs of a debate happening in the background. In 1791

6. Hindmarsh, *Rise and Progress*, 70–71.

7. This incident led Wesley's brother Charles to write a poem that encapsulates the problem that many saw: "So easily are bishops made / By man or woman's whim / W his hands on C has laid / But who laid hands on him?" Vickers, *Thomas Coke*, 101.

the conference, "having examined the proceedings of the London Society," unanimously confirmed them and recognized James Hindmarsh, Joseph Wright, Manoah Sibly, Francis Leicester, and Robert Jackson as ministers of the New Jerusalem "fully authorized to officiate in the character of priests."[8] In 1807, the account of the first ordinations in the minute book was read out, and it was resolved that it should be "considered the most consistent, proper and expedient according to the then existing circumstances."[9]

The 1807 conference, the first since 1793, had been proposed by three ministers (Joseph Proud, Manoah Sibly, and James Hodson), who, according to Henry Servanté, were "tinctured with some of the old Papal leaven of priestly supremacy" and wanted the conference to confirm that only ordained ministers could conduct further ordinations:

> The intended purport of the Conference is, I understand, on the question of Ordination, which, if brought forward in the way these three gentlemen wish to assume, would, I apprehend, occasion much dissatisfaction; because I doubt much whether they can come to any conclusion that would satisfy the friends in general, or that the writings of ES will bear them out; for Swedenborg has given no directions upon that subject; indicating, in my opinion, that all societies are free to adopt what rituals they may think proper. . . . Neither Mr Clowes nor any other clergymen will acknowledge the assumed and indisputable right of London to ordain, and I, for one, trust they never may; for it would be introducing a Papal New Church authority, and will be that of any other. One society has not the shadow of right to dictate to another upon its formalities; and if it does, it is wholly from proprium and to service dominion. James, the father of Robert Hindmarsh, after his ordination some years ago at Eastcheap, aimed at this authority, for which he justly obtained the nickname of Bishop of Babylon.[10]

Shortly after the conference, an anonymous pamphlet (probably written by J. A. Tulk) was published, which argued strongly against the propriety of the New Church ordinations. It argued that the old church began in perfection and subsequently declined while the New Church will rise from that state of imperfection. Just as the laity will be collected from the laity of the old church, so the clergy will be drawn from the clergy of the old church.

8. Anon., *Minutes of the First*, 70.

9. Boyle, "Historic Notice," xvii.

10. Servanté, "Epistolary Correspondence IV," 281.

> The present ordination of teachers, in the most apologising view, can only be considered as the temporary substitution of non-real thing for the real thing, until, in the Divine Order and progression toward the perfect state of the Church, the true and real clergy, namely, the present preparing Clergy of the Old Church shall be called forth of Divine Providence, in due season, to the regular exercise of the function of ministerial office . . . let not the members of the New Church be deceived with the idea that these laical appointments constitute the real Clergy of the New Church, much less than the source of that Clergy, and that such lay substitutes are or can be sanctioned to ordain to the office, when they themselves are sanctioned by no new Divine Appointment whatever.[11]

This was precisely the opposite of Robert's argument, that the New Church was new and so could not be subject to the authority of the old and therefore ordination had to come from within.

Notwithstanding these differences of view, the propriety of the first ordinations was again reaffirmed in 1808. Then, at the conference of 1818, there was a long discussion, after which it was resolved unanimously

> that in consequence of Mr Robert Hindmarsh having been called by Lot to ordain the first Minister in the New Church, this Conference consider it as the most orderly method, which could then be adopted, and that Mr Robert Hindmarsh was virtually Ordained by the Divine Auspices of Heaven; in consequence of which this Conference consider Mr Robert Hindmarsh as one of the regular Ordaining Ministers.[12]

Thereafter Robert's name came at the top of any list of ministers in the New Church, and in the column "ordained by" it said "the divine auspices of heaven" in place of the name of the presiding minister.

There is another account of that first ordination, by Manoah Sibly, one of the first ordained ministers after James Hindmarsh and Samuel Smith and one of those chosen by lot. He relates that twelve of the lottery papers contained the word "ordain" while just one had "a particular mark," and Boyle comments that the original Great Eastcheap minutes include a note in the margin in Robert's handwriting:

11. Layman, "Plain Observations," 5.
12. Anon., *Minutes of the Eleventh*, 19.

> NB—A particular mark was made on one of the lots, appointing the person to read on whom it should fall, and it fell on Robert Hindmarsh.[13]

This small difference could be significant: Robert's account in *Rise and Progress*, where just one lottery paper contained the word "ordain" and he refers to his father as "ordained by me," could imply that he regarded himself alone as performing the ordination, while Sibly's account (and Robert's marginal note) imply that all of the chosen twelve performed the act, with one person being appointed just to read the service. Furthermore, the ordination service as recorded in the minute book states that "ordination into the Priesthood is effected by the Imposition of Hands," something that all twelve participants did. Some see this as evidence that Robert changed his account of that day in order to emphasize his own role and support the 1818 conference resolution. Sibly goes as far as to claim that Robert himself considered these events made his own ordination unnecessary:

> These circumstances were not known at the time, nor did they transpire for several years afterwards, when he mentioned them himself as reasons for not undergoing the ceremony of ordination, like the other ministers of the Lord's New Church, conceiving himself hereby to be equally, yea superiorly ordained to the ministerial office.[14]

Odhner, probably following Sibly, agreed with this:

> Robert Hindmarsh, in consequence, considered himself doubly chosen, by the Lord himself as well as by the Church, to act as the principal ordainer, and that he himself, in fact, and by virtue of this double choice, was ordained a priest of the New Jerusalem.[15]

Elihu Rich, the author of *A Biographical Sketch of Emanuel Swedenborg* in 1849, makes an explicit connection with the lottery, suggesting that the fact that "ordain" was written on one of papers means that Robert thought that he alone was doing the ordaining.[16]

There is some evidence from *Rise and Progress* that Robert considered himself specially chosen. He states that he was "chosen by lot, as well as by the unanimous voice of the members of the Society assembled for that

13. Boyle, "Historic Notice," xv.
14. Boyle, "Historic Notice," xiv.
15. Odhner, *Robert Hindmarsh*, 21–22.
16. Rich, "Early History," 544.

purpose, to ordain his father, Mr James Hindmarsh, as a Minister," clearly referring to the special lottery paper,[17] and his account of the ordination service refers to him having been chosen to perform the ordination of his father and Samuel Smith. However, it is far less clear that either he or the wider church considered him to have been actually ordained by these events. At the 1793 conference in Great Eastcheap, the minutes state that "the senior minister," James Hindmarsh, took the chair and Robert was appointed secretary. If the conference had thought Robert had been ordained, he would surely have been regarded as the senior minister. Furthermore, between that first ordination ceremony and the 1818 conference, Robert took no part in any ordination ceremony and is always referred to as simply "Mr Hindmarsh" in all the church's literature.[18] Nor did he appear in any list of ministers until the 1818 conference. In *Rise and Progress*, Robert writes that the temple at Cross Street, Hatton Garden was kept open "by the assistance of several individuals *not then in the Ministry*,"[19] and both Sibly[20] and Proud[21] indicate that Robert was one of those individuals. In a letter written in 1817, Robert wrote,

> With respect to my entrance into the ministry, it is true, that I officiate as a minister; but do not consider myself permanently fixed in that character. A variety of circumstances concurred to bring me into my present situation, among which were chiefly the repeated solicitations of several friends in this town, who thought I might be useful in a public capacity. To these solicitations I yielded, as it were only for the present: and I have gone in this way now between five and six years, yet without any ceremony of ordination having passed over me. The ordination established in the New Church in this kingdom, commenced in London, I think, about the year 1788; and it was the unanimous wish of the society, and at the same time a decision by lot, unknown to them, that I should read the ordination service. From that beginning the ordinations have succeeded regularly; but still there are many, who officiate as leaders, and even as ministers, who have not been introduced

17. Hindmarsh, *Rise and Progress*, 72.

18. Boyle, "Historic Notice," xi.

19. Hindmarsh, *Rise and Progress*, 173 (my italics).

20. Sibly, "Address," 5. Sibly's address can also be found in Robinson, *Remembrancer and Recorder*, 110–15.

21. Proud, "Memoirs," 16. The page number refers to the typescript copy of the original manuscript in the library of the Swedenborg Society in London.

> by ordination; and the services of such are found highly useful in various places, especially in small country villages.[22]

So we have Sibly, who knew Robert very well (though was on the other side of a later split in the New Church), and Odhner (writing over one hundred years later) saying that Robert considered himself to be ordained; while the behavior of the church, Robert referring to himself "not then in the ministry," and the letter from Robert clearly stating "no ceremony of ordination [had] passed over me" suggesting otherwise. Equally, Robert's reference to his status as not being permanently fixed and his letter in 1817 do not suggest that he felt any particular need to be pronounced as ordained.

The conference resolutions did not finally settle the issue, as arguments over the first ordinations and the declaration of Robert's ordination broke out several times during the 1800s. Indeed, by 1905 James Hyde could refer to Robert's ordination as a "fiction" without feeling the need to justify the remark.[23] The argument centered on three issues: the use of the lot; the authority, or lack of it, of the chosen twelve; and the propriety of the declaration of Robert's ordination.

The use of the lot was criticized on the grounds that divine providence could equally well have influenced a rational discussion and that the specific manner of its use in effect constrained the divine will; there was no opportunity for the divine will to say "ordain no one," for example. It was also argued that their use of the lot was more closely related to modern parallels, such as in Methodism or the Moravians, than it was to biblical precedents. William Mason went further and argued that the first ordinations were not merely misguided but immoral too. God had not provided any promise or covenant to guide them by the use of the lot, and so they had no right to ask for such guidance. He pointed out that Robert had self-confessedly marked the twelfth paper for his own private satisfaction and so his selection of that lot could provide nothing other than self-ordination. He even suggests that, had someone else chosen that paper, Robert would still have claimed divine appointment and considered that the people had chosen wrongly. Mason was also unconvinced by the ability of those present to know what they were actually doing:

> I personally knew four of the lot-selected twelve, and I do not believe they were, from the simplicity of their character, at all fitted

22. Hindmarsh, "Letter of Rev," 102.

23. Hyde, "Some Notes II," 118.

> to decide whether the proceeding was proper or not. One of them was actually a night street watchman, and not a moral man, by any means.[24]

Notwithstanding this harsh judgment, Mason acknowledges a different source of authority for the ordinations and finds room to praise Robert in general:

> I affirm that in propriety of speech, the lot ordination was not the origin of the [New Church] ministry. The origin was the honest intention to carry out the Divine commission above referred to [i.e., "Go and teach to all nations."]; the "lotting" was a sad piece of chance medley very improperly connected with the carrying out of this intention.[25]

Mason goes on to say, "The silly proceedings resorted to by Mr H does not in the least overshadow to me the nobleness of his character.[26]

As well as the use of the lot being criticized, the authority of the twelve was denied, not least because most of them hadn't even been baptized in the New Church: who were they to set themselves up as the creators of a new priesthood, let alone determine that priesthood for other societies? The fact that some of them had been Methodist preachers was irrelevant, as they had not been ordained and had simply been permitted by Wesley to preach; there was no continuity of apostolic succession. If the New Church was in the twelve, they were guilty of schism; if it was not then they had no rationale to act as they did.[27] As for Robert, even accepting the process of choosing, he was merely designated as the person to read the service and nothing more. As the service itself proclaims, ordination is through the laying on of hands and not the reading of a service, and no one laid hands on Robert.

An extraordinary undated and anonymous manuscript in the library of the Swedenborg Society[28] declares that *Rise and Progress* is biased and that the author wishes to set out the facts. He or she regards the ordination

24. Mason, "Origin," 44.

25. Mason, "Origin," 41.

26. Mason, "Origin," 45.

27. Delta, "On the Use"; Rich, "Early History."

28. The author may be James Hyde. The handwriting does not match that of Charles Higham, the other prominent New Church historian of the time, but it is similar to that of James Hyde in a notebook that appears to be a first draft of his articles in the *New Church Magazine* in 1905.

by the divine auspices of heaven to be "the crowning proof of the strange megalomania of an ambitious, aggressive and many-sided nature."[29] While ordination in the early new church was necessary for the sake of good order, the

> unfortunate acceptance of Hindmarsh's invalid claim defaced the church's records with one of the most repugnant and irreverent decisions ever chronicled in the annals of professing Christians. . . . What disturbs one most is the reflection that through close on fifty years this man eminent and estimable in so many ways could so yield to his own egotism as to distort the evidence of his own hand and could make claims in his latter days which the testimony of his beloved contemporary eyewitness Manoah Sibly prove to be impossible.[30]

The manuscript takes the view that Robert, driven by self-aggrandizement, sought out the ruling on his own ordination and distorted the account of the first ordination to that end. This seems a rather harsh judgment on Robert as there is no written evidence that he ever claimed to have in effect been ordained that day in 1788. Changing his account of the lottery from "a particular mark" to the word "ordain," assuming it was deliberate, only takes you half way there: you still have to accept that having been chosen by lot to ordain meant that he himself was *de facto* ordained and that he was responsible for the ordination rather than it being the twelve, as the ordination service (written by Robert) states.

In response to these criticisms of the first ordinations, the main argument was that the whole affair was a simple practical expedient: the New Church needed an ordained ministry, and this was a way of getting one. Furthermore, apostolic succession back to Jesus couldn't be traced in history, and so a break in the supposed succession was not an issue.[31] Others suggested that it was odd to appeal to the old church when considering how the New Church should be organized. Robert Abbott, a New Church minister writing in the 1880s, acknowledged the controversy but argued that there was little else that Hindmarsh and the others could have done if they were to initiate a new ministry that was not founded in the old church and that countenanced divine providence. He suggested that some of those who

29. Anon., "R Hindmarsh."

30. Anon., "R Hindmarsh."

31. Mason, "Origin"; Firmitas, "On Ordination"; Investigator, "On Ordination."

criticized Robert did so out of presbyterian prejudice rather than justified objection. He summarized the events of the first ordination and continued,

> Such are the simple facts, surely not unworthy of the important crisis. The decision derives no force from worldly distinction or worldly wisdom: and in this there is a resemblance to the appointment of the first Christian ministry. The entire absence of anything like ecclesiastical authority, the conscientious recognition of the finger of Providence, and the spirit of meekness and charity in which the ceremonial was carried out, invest the whole transaction with singular fitness and completeness, which commanded the acquiescence in subsequent deliberations.[32]

Where the various writers were placed in this debate depended largely on their view of ordination. Those who took a high view of ordination, that it was a ceremony that passed something tangible down through apostolic succession from the first disciples of Jesus to create a priestly class who were set apart from others, tended to argue that the Great Eastcheap ordinations in 1788 were a sham. Those who took a low view of ordination, that it was simply a means of recognizing some individuals as fit for a particular service to the church, tended to argue that the Great Eastcheap ordinations were a practical response to a specific situation and just as valid as any other ordinations. Naturally, both sides tried to use Swedenborg's writings to justify their stance.

But what of Robert's supposed ordination "by the divine auspices of heaven"? On the last day of the 1818 conference, in response to requests from several societies for a clear opinion, it resolved

> that it appears to this Conference, after mature deliberation, that the administering of these ordinances [i.e., baptism and the Lord's Supper] belong properly to the ministry: nevertheless it is not hereby meant to pass a censure on those leaders of societies, who have heretofore been, and still are, in the habit of administering either the ceremony of baptism or the holy supper, having good reason to believe, that they have in such cases, acted uprightly and conscientiously.[33]

While the resolution carefully avoided criticizing what had happened in the past, it would change who would be able to continue to administer the ceremonies. And this created a problem. Robert, the elected president

32. Abbott, "Establishment," 151–52.

33. Anon., *Minutes of the Eleventh*, 18.

of the 1818 conference, had been a minister in Salford for some six years at the time, carrying out various sacraments and ceremonies, including baptism and burial, and presumably "the holy supper" too. The resolution effectively deprived him, one of their most prominent and distinguished ministers, of his job. A solution had to be found, and so Robert was asked to leave the room, and "the ordination of Mr Robert Hindmarsh was then introduced, and underwent a very deliberate and able discussion." The result of this "deliberate and able discussion" was to declare that Robert had, unbeknown to everyone, actually been ordained many years before. So everything was just fine after all.

Whether Robert really believed he had been ordained in 1788 or had any influence on the decision of the conference has been lost to history, though the balance of evidence is that he probably did not. All we know for sure is that Robert was out of the room while the discussion and formulation of the resolution took place. One can imagine him being aware of the resolution on baptisms and the holy supper and thinking, in effect, "hang on a minute, this means I have to be ordained or it will put me out of a job." Then maybe one of his supporters, recalling the 1788 ceremony and the fact that Robert had been chosen by lot to lead those who laid hands on James Hindmarsh and Samuel Smith, suggested that, if only ordained ministers can ordain, then Robert must have had the status of being ordained back in 1788. Thus the resolution on the ministry could stand, no one would be offended or cast aside, and everyone would be satisfied. This happy solution may have been aided by the fact that none of the other sixteen present in 1788 were among those attending the 1818 conference.

6

Sex and Schism

Having established a new church with a building in which to worship and a form of ministry, the Society for Promoting the Heavenly Doctrines of the New Jerusalem Church decided to organize a conference. It was announced in a circular letter signed by eight members of the society, including Robert, who was secretary and treasurer, and was almost certainly printed by Robert too. As the letter makes clear, the conference was primarily called to further the cause of separation:

> At a full Meeting of the Members of the New Church, it was unanimously resolved, to call a General Conference, for the purpose of considering the most effectual Means to promote the Establishment of the New Church distinct from the Old, to be held at Great East Cheap, London, on the 27th Day of January next [1789], being the Anniversary of the Opening of the said New Jerusalem Church.[1]

The conference was opened with a welcome speech by Robert and was largely concerned with passing thirty-one resolutions giving doctrinal definition to the New Church. This included a clear resolution that the faith of the old church

1. Quoted in Hindmarsh, *Rise and Progress*, 80.

> ought to be abolished from the Mind of every Individual, in Order that the Faith of the New Church may gain Admission and be established.[2]

No less than five of the resolutions were concerned with repudiating the traditional doctrine of the Trinity or expounding that of the New Church, which is unsurprising given how Swedenborg's approach to the Trinity had been central to Robert's and others' thinking. The resolutions emphasized the rationality of the new faith, asserting that it was "consistent with sound rationality" and that separation from the old church will arise from "rational conviction," and hence distanced the New Church from popular mystical stereotypes of Swedenborg.[3] And there was a resolution introducing a political dimension to the views of the New Church:

> [The writings of Swedenborg] are calculated to promote the Peace and Happiness of Mankind, by making them Loyal Subjects, Lovers of their Country, and useful members of Society: And therefore that these Resolutions are not intended to militate against, or in the smallest Degree to annul the civil Authority in any Country; but only to emancipate Mankind from the mental Bondage and Slavery, wherein they have too long been held captive by the Leaders and Rulers in the Old Church.[4]

This was probably a defensive resolution, designed to ensure that no one could accuse the New Church of being in any way seditious. This influence of the politics of the time, and Robert's politics in particular, on the developing New Church will be discussed at length in chapter 8, which considers how it became a major factor in a dispute at the fourth General Conference.

Robert's role in the conference is interesting: he was not elected president or secretary of the conference and he was not one of the fourteen signatories of the minutes, yet he was "directed by the members of the New Jerusalem Church in London"[5] to open the conference and welcome the attendees. He was clearly a central figure, but not necessarily through holding positions of formal authority.

Robert records that some sixty to seventy members, male and female, were present and that

2. Anon., *Minutes of the First*, 33.
3. Deck, "Blake and Swedenborg," 306–7.
4. Anon., *Minutes of the First*, 41–42.
5. Anon., *Minutes of the First*, 4.

> although the individuals composing it came from the east, the west, the north, and the south, and had been previously of almost every denomination of professing Christians, such was the unanimity which prevailed on all the subjects of discussion, that not a single dissenting voice was heard, but the whole of the proceedings was conducted in harmony, peace, and love.[6]

However, the harmony did not last long, as soon after the 1789 conference there was a conflict that resulted in the expulsion of Robert and five others from the Great Eastcheap society. Manoah Sibly hints at what happened:

> I am here under the necessity of stating, however reluctantly, that in the year 1789 a very sorrowful occurrence befell the infant New Church, whereby the flood-gates of immorality were in danger of being thrown open, to her inevitable destruction. The Church held many solemn meetings on the occasion, which ended in her withdrawing herself from six of her members, viz: Robert Hindmarsh, Henry Servanté, Charles Berns Wadström, August Nordenskjöld, George Robinson, and Alexander Wilderspin.[7]

The Great Eastcheap congregation "held many solemn meetings," but at some point they or someone else chose to hide them from history, as the pages of the Great Eastcheap minute book between May 4, 1789 and April 11, 1790 were removed, and they do not appear in a copy of the minute book either. So what was it that threatened to open the "floodgates of immorality"?

The original edition of the *Dictionary of National Biography* entry for Robert Hindmarsh rather coyly describes the expulsion as being "on the ground of lax views of the conjugal relation, perhaps only theoretical,"[8] but a more detailed explanation emerged as a by-product of one of the periodic bouts of argument over the first ordinations in the New Church. In 1852, Elihu Rich drew attention to the pamphlet by Manoah Sibly (from which the above quote came) in order to demonstrate that Robert was a fallible human being. No New Church ministry could be founded on such an individual, and therefore the ordinations themselves were invalidated.[9] In response, John Isaac Hawkins (thought to be the oldest then-living

6. Hindmarsh, *Rise and Progress*, 105.
7. Sibly, "Address."
8. Gordon, "Hindmarsh," 2.
9. Rich, "Early History."

member of the New Church, and son of Isaac Hawkins, one of the first New Church ministers and friend of James Hindmarsh) explained the nature of the dispute:

> With respect to the sorrowful occurrence you allude to . . . it was a perverted view of Swedenborg's doctrine of concubinage, in his work on Conjugial Love, then just published; whereby some held that if a husband and wife did not agree, they might separate, and the man take a concubine; I forget whether or not the wife was to have the same privilege.[10]

This was confirmed by another correspondent:

> The evil itself was no other than an erroneous view of Swedenborg's teachings in the treatise on Scortatory Love—a work which was viewed from an unchaste ground by some of the early receivers of the doctrines and abused to the shame of those bodies which were intended to be temples of the Holy Spirit.[11]

Swedenborg had set out his views on these matters in his *Delights of Wisdom Concerning Conjugial Love: After Which Follow Pleasures of Insanity Concerning Scortatory Love*. His view of marriage was very high: conjugial love, the love that occurs between a husband and wife in a chaste marriage, has its origins in the marriage of truth and good in heaven and corresponds to the marriage of the Lord with the church. Adultery was its very opposite, as it destroyed the conjugial love of marriage. Because of its heavenly origin, conjugial love can only exist in those who come to the Lord, and the extent of conjugial love depends on the state of the church within them. This latter point is crucial, as Swedenborg did not take the view that conjugial love was all or nothing. There were degrees to it and therefore degrees to its absence; the world is an imperfect place and does not always conform to the heavenly ideal. Swedenborg recognized that people (well, men at least) cannot always live up to the ideal and may have sexual desires they cannot control. He argues that the tolerance of brothels by a wide range of countries, kings, and authorities is to prevent greater evils that might arise if they did not exist.[12] Similarly, sex with a married woman (i.e., adultery) is worse than with an unmarried woman (in Swedenborg's

10. Quoted in Warren, "Rev Robert Hindmarsh Vindicated," 143–44.

11. Bateman, "Letter," 145.

12. Swedenborg, *Delights of Wisdom*, 416–17.

language, fornication with a harlot).[13] He goes so far as to describe three "spheres"[14]: conjugial love, fornication, and scortatory love (i.e., adultery), of which fornication is the middle one. Indeed, for a man who is not yet ready or able to be married, he argued that it would be better for him to take a single mistress (who is neither married nor a virgin) than allow free reign to his lust, as this would allow the possibility of conjugial love in the future to be maintained.[15] For the married, there were circumstances in which it was legitimate to separate from a wife and take a concubine while maintaining conjugial love. These circumstances included

> madness, frenzy, furious wildness, actual foolishness and idiotism, loss of memory, violent hysterics, extreme simpleness so as to admit of no perception of good and truth, an high degree of stubbornness in refusing to obey what is just and equitable; an high degree of pleasure in talkativeness and discoursing only on insignificant and trifling subjects; an unbridled desire to publish family secrets, also to quarrel, to strike, to take revenge, to do evil, to steal, to tell lies, to deceive, to blaspheme; carelessness about the children, intemperance, luxury, excessive prodigality, drunkenness, uncleanness, immodesty, application to magic and witchcraft, impiety, with several other causes.[16]

Swedenborg's *Conjugial Love* had been published in Amsterdam in Latin in 1768 and was first translated into English by John Clowes (and printed by Robert) in 1794, so it was probably not widely known among the early Swedenborgians in 1789. Those who could read Latin would be able to consult the work, but the rest would have had to rely on secondhand views of its contents.

The dispute probably arose when Augustus Nordenskjöld presented a comprehensive plan of church governance to the Eastcheap society.[17] Among other things, the plan was democratic and allowed women as well as men to take part in the election of representatives. However, it was the discussion of concubinage (which formed only a small part of the plan—the last of fifty-four paragraphs) which caused the controversy: Nordenskjöld interpreted *Conjugial Love* as meaning that a marriage was only genuine

13. Swedenborg, *Delights of Wisdom*, 412.
14. Swedenborg, *Delights of Wisdom*, 419.
15. Swedenborg, *Delights of Wisdom*, 421.
16. Swedenborg, *Delights of Wisdom*, 245.
17. Paley, "New Heaven Begun," 71.

if it was within the New Church and that a man could take a concubine if his wife did not accept the Swedenborgian doctrines. He also added an institutional control:

> It will happen, of course, that for a long time to come there will be unmarried men in our Church who will not be able to marry, and married men who have been received among us, but who have unchristian wives, rejecting the New Doctrine, and who thus must live in a disharmonious marriage, it follows that when such men are driven so strongly by the inborn *amor sexus* that they cannot contain themselves, it is inevitable, for the sake of order, that they be permitted, the former to take a mistress and the latter a concubine. But no one is permitted to live thus in our Church who does not report it to the Bishop or the Marriage-Priest.[18]

Nordenskjöld's view is not explicitly stated in Swedenborg's writings but was clearly derived from them. Notwithstanding this, it was all too much for the more conservative English members of the society. James Hindmarsh was so distracted by the controversy that he failed to prepare a sermon one Sunday and read out the Sermon on the Mount instead.[19] John Clowes recalled an occasion when two Swedish gentlemen (the other being Wadström) had presented a plan of worship, the contents of which were

> opposed to every sentiment of propriety, decorum and common sense of mankind, [and] were pressed on the members of the Church in this extraordinary plan, as of divine authority.[20]

James Hindmarsh, as a former Methodist preacher, would have been well aware of the various attacks on Methodist morality and sexuality. The emphasis on emotion, desire, urgency, and sensation in evangelical worship could be regarded as highly sexualized, particularly when set alongside the swooning, shuddering, and weeping of an ecstatic congregation. Methodist preachers were vulnerable to suspicion about sexual misdemeanors with itinerancy being seen as enabling preachers to leave behind illegitimate children and abandoned women. Some preachers were expelled from Methodism for adultery, and seduction by Methodist preachers became a popular literary trope. One result was that Methodists and other evangelicals were highly concerned about self-control and saw this as essential to both

18. Nordenskjöld, "Församlings Formen," translation quoted in Paley, "A New Heaven," 71.

19. Bateman, "Letter," 145.

20. Letter of Sept. 11, 1820, quoted in Deck, "Blake and Swedenborg."

personal and social morality. At the same time, the 1780s saw an increasing desire for moral reform. New generations of converts combined their obligation of self-appraisal with a desire to improve society (and thereby avoid any falling back into unredeemed ways). The family, in particular, was seen as a primary location for morality, with its child-rearing role and hierarchical structure; a godly family and household was the most effective way to control the disruptive aspects of sexuality. Even marital sex was regarded as something that needed regulating, as there were concerns that unregulated sex by laboring men led to families too large for them (or the nation's food supply) to support, with the answer being moral restraint. In 1787 King George III had joined the call for moral reform with a *Proclamation for the Encouragement of Piety and Virtue, and for the Prevention and Punishing of Vice, Profaneness and Immorality*, which called for the suppression of all "loose and licentious Prints, Books, and Publications, dispersing Poison to the minds of the Young and Unwary." The aim was to protect the rising generation from the lure of "indelicate literature and pornography."[21]

Against this background it is unsurprising that many of the early Swedenborgians had trouble accepting Nordenskjöld's views despite them being derived from Swedenborg's writings. Robert and the other five who were expelled must have accepted some of it and, at least in Robert's case, he would have had the benefit of being able to read *Conjugial Love* in the original Latin as well. It was said that August Nordenskjöld acted upon his views,[22] but there is no evidence that Robert or any of the others did. As Samuel Warren wrote,

> the notion soon ceased to be broached, and the Church was relieved from further discussion of the distressing subject. I do not recollect any case when the notion was acted on. Mr Hindmarsh certainly did not; nor do I believe that either of the other five persons you name did.[23]

Henry Bateman agreed:

> Whilst Robert Hindmarsh believed that those views were true to some extent, and to a degree which was calculated in the estimation of good Mr. Sibly to open "the flood gates of immorality," he kept aloof in the opinion of Mr. Sibly himself from all unchaste

21. Quoted in Gibson and Begiato, *Sex and the Church*, 283.

22. Letter of Thomas Dawes to the Swedenborg Society in 1842, quoted in Tafel, *Documents*, 807.

23. Warren, "Rev Robert Hindmarsh Vindicated," 144.

> practices, and was thus preserved from that worst of confirmations an evil life.... How soon Mr Robert Hindmarsh got rid of his erroneous impressions, as to Swedenborg's teaching, I know not, but as he was not a man to conceal his sentiments, and never afterwards, so far as I am aware, expressed his concurrence in these notions which we have had adverted to, we may fairly conclude that he was speedily delivered from them by the Lord whom he loved.[24]

There is something of an irony in a sect established by Robert's sectarian zeal employing its sectarianism to expel him.

In 1820 the Rev. J. G. Pike published a broadside against the New Church, *Swedenborgianism Depicted in Its True Colours*,[25] and the conference that year requested that Robert write a response. Part of Pike's critique centered on *Conjugial Love* and essentially accused the New Church of encouraging vice and adultery. Robert's response,[26] drawing directly on Swedenborg, said, among other things:

- Swedenborg argues strongly against fornication and adultery, but there are degrees of evil and not all examples of fornication or adultery are of the same degree.
- True and faithful marriage corresponds to the marriage of the Lord with the church and so is pure and holy. However, not everyone can live up to this standard, and so Swedenborg seeks to identify cases where some falling short might prevent a greater evil. He nowhere approves of fornication or adultery.
- Concubinage with a wife and apart from a wife are very different. The former is detestable, the latter, when engaged in with just causes, may not be so. Swedenborg gives some cases where it may be just.
- Quoting from Swedenborg: "if the man, who has been living in a state of fornication, converts himself to conjugial love, that is, to a love truly spiritual, as being derived from the Lord himself, he thus converts himself to heaven."[27]
- A repeat of Swedenborg's argument about the toleration of brothels.

24. Bateman, "Letter," 145.
25. Pike, *Swedenborgianism Depicted.*
26. Hindmarsh, *Vindication.*
27. Hindmarsh, *Vindication*, 194–95.

The argument is very faithful to Swedenborg and shows that Robert almost certainly did not abandon the views that led to his expulsion, even if he never acted on them or particularly promoted them. The claim that Swedenborg nowhere approves of fornication or adultery is moot—it rather depends on whether accepting one or other as a lesser evil in some circumstances counts as approval or not—but this may have been a formulation that allowed the New Church to remain in line with common morality while not disavowing Swedenborg. Also, Robert does not quote some of the more explicit passages, such as where Swedenborg allows an unmarried man to take a mistress. However, it is clear that Robert was following Swedenborg's more nuanced view of sexual relations in which there are shades of grey rather than absolutes. Nordenskjöld may well have been more provocative in his presentation in 1789, but Robert clearly thought he was being essentially true to Swedenborg and that is why he was part of the group that was expelled.

Underlying all this was probably a difference of view of the authority of Swedenborg's writings. Roger Bernet, writing in 1799,[28] divided Swedenborgians into two groups: those who regard the writings as the word of God like the Gospels, and those who saw them as highly illuminated by God but not on a par with the Gospels. Robert took a very high view of their authority—as he said about his second encounter with the writings, he saw them as having a heavenly origin—and so probably fell into the first group. As a result he saw this heavenly authority as being at stake in the dispute and felt obliged to follow Swedenborg's writings in all things, even when they departed from the common morality of the day. The émigré followers, such as Nordenskjöld and Wadström, with their more radical backgrounds, were probably more comfortable with such views, but few of the English evangelicals could tolerate them, despite their clarity in Swedenborg's writings.

As mentioned in chapter 3, it seems likely that some of those expelled met together (perhaps with some others) on August 23, 1789 to form the Universal London Society for the Promotion of the New Jerusalem Church (whose constitution included a statement about the accurate translation and speedy printing of *Conjugial Love*) and to publish *The New Jerusalem Magazine*. The magazine published part of Nordenskjöld's plan in 1790, though omitting the more controversial paragraph on concubinage.

28. Bernet, "To the Editors," 235.

Robert's expulsion did not dim his enthusiasm for the New Church or, it seems, his acceptance as part of the broader community of Swedenborgians. As Sibly commented,

> I wish to mention here, to the honour of Mr Robert Hindmarsh, that, notwithstanding he discontinued to be a member of the Society, there was no breach of personal friendship between him and the members of the society; he still held the joint tenancy of the place, and attended, as usual, the meetings of the Church for public worship, as well as for business; and did all in his power to promote the establishment of the New Church distinct from the old Church; and the Society were much gratified herewith, conceiving him to be a very valuable man, possessing a bright understanding, and a devout well-wisher for her prosperity. The Church, therefore, went on pretty comfortably, with Robert Hindmarsh generally present among them.[29]

This is undoubtedly correct, as we find Robert attended nearly half of the business meetings of the Great Eastcheap society from when the minute book resumes in 1790 until it finishes in 1791. He was also present at the second conference in 1790 and, while not holding office, was one of seven people appointed to write a letter to the various societies around the country. He was clearly continuing a prominent role in the movement despite his apparent expulsion.

The others, however, did not. Wilderspin and Robinson both disappear from New Church records after their expulsion. Henry Servanté played no further role in London Swedenborgianism other than his involvement with the Universal London Society and *The New Jerusalem Magazine*, and a letter of 1805[30] implies that he held to the same views. Nordenskjöld left London in the middle of 1790, and Wadström became increasingly involved in opposition to the slave trade and left for France in 1795. Thus there were three responses to the expulsions: continue more or less as though they had never happened (Robert); form another society in which their views were acceptable (Servanté, Nordenskjöld, and Wadström); or take umbrage and disappear altogether (Wilderspin and Robinson). Robert was perhaps too personally invested in the Great Eastcheap society to walk away completely, and his joint tenancy of the building also gave him a financial stake in its affairs. He probably had too little in common with Servanté et al.,

29. Sibly, "Address."

30. Servanté, "Epistolary Correspondence II," 313.

and certainly with Nordenskjöld's views on church government, to have joined the more radical group. As Sibly remarks, the society considered him a valuable presence, and so it seems it was prepared to tolerate his continuing involvement.

Conjugial Love continued to be a problem for the New Church, creating a target for its opponents and a focus of dispute within. There was even a major legal case arising from the will of F. J. Kramph, who left a legacy for the foundation of a university for the New Church in Philadelphia, USA. This legacy was claimed by the Academy of the New Church, an institution founded by a branch of the New Church and not connected to the general convention in the United States, but this claim was disputed by others on the grounds that the Academy was not a fit and proper institution. The reason was that the Academy upheld the teaching of *Conjugial Love*, which was deemed repugnant and offensive to public policy. The case went all the way to the Supreme Court of Pennsylvania where it was eventually decided in favor of the Academy. The ruling was not on the doctrine itself but on whether the doctrine was a reason to negate the Kramph will, but the underlying argument was essentially the same as in 1789 in London. A lengthy account of the history of the controversy and the Kramph will case commented that,

> from all the evidence, together with the known attitude of Hindmarsh and his associates toward the Writings, it is manifest that they simply upheld the Divine Authority of the Doctrine.[31]

31. Anon., *Kramph*.

7

More Conferences and Joseph Priestley

The following year, at the second General Conference in 1790, Robert once again had little formal role. He was neither president nor secretary, nor a signatory to the minutes, though he was part of a small group appointed to enact the business of the conference and one of seven signatories to a letter accompanying the minutes. The conference was primarily concerned with two issues. First, whether a form of prayer ought to be used in religious worship in the New Church (the conference decided that it should) and, second, a revision of the order of worship that had been drawn up and printed by the Great Eastcheap society. The conference also agreed that "in order to open the gates of the New Jerusalem as wide as possible" the only condition of admission by baptism to the New Church should be an acknowledgment of two essentials of the New Church:

> I. That God is One both in Essence and a Person, in whom is a Divine Trinity, consisting of Father, Son, and Holy Spirit, that the Lord and Saviour Jesus Christ is He. II. That in Order to Salvation Man must live a Life according to the Ten Commandments, by shunning Evils as Sins against God.[1]

By the third General Conference, in 1791, Robert's rehabilitation was complete and he was elected secretary of the conference and a member of the committee to enact the business of the conference. It was as peaceful

1. Boyle, "Historic Notice," 56.

as the first two, but this time only receivers of Swedenborg doctrines who supported separation were admitted as members and permitted to speak. On the first day the Minutes record the first sign of disagreement over the status of ministers in the New Church:

> Mr Samuel Hands, after noticing the Evils that had arisen in the Old Church, in Consequence of the Clergy assuming to themselves the Rights and Privileges above the Laity, in matters of spiritual or religious Inquiry, requested that the Conference would take such Measures as they thought most likely to prevent the Introduction of such Abuses into the New Church. He accordingly made a Motion to that Effect, which being duly seconded, it was unanimously Resolved, that in all Consultations and Deliberations of this Conference, no Privileges shall be attached to the Clergy in Preference to the Laity, but that in all Respects whatever they shall be on an equal footing.[2]

Despite this motion against priestly privileges, the conference also endorsed an elaborate form of dress for its ministers:

> An Inner Purple Silken Vest, and also an outer Garment of fine White Linen, having a golden Girdle around the Breast.[3]

In response it was proposed that some general rules for the government of the New Church be drawn up and brought before the next conference. These issues, the role of the clergy and the form of government of the New Church, were to become a major source of conflict the following year, with Robert, as usual, playing a central role.

Meanwhile, Samuel Hands also proposed that the Great Eastcheap society should form itself into a proper body with officers appointed for its management. He suggested that other societies would naturally follow the lead of the London society and so the New Church would become properly organized. The members at Great Eastcheap, including Robert, withdrew to consider this and returned with a resolution acknowledging themselves as members:

> We, the Undersigned, wishing Peace to all Men, and all spiritual and temporal Blessings to our lawful King, George the Third, his Royal Family, and all concerned in the Government of his Dominions, where, by the Mercy of the Lord, we are favoured with

2. Anon., *Minutes of the First*, 64.
3. Anon., *Minutes of the First*, 67.

> the Protection of the Laws, justly administered, to secure to us the Enjoyment of all our religious and civil Liberties, hereby acknowledge ourselves Members of the New Church in Great East Cheap, London.[4]

Robinson, writing much later, in 1862, notes the oddity of the resolution, which professes loyalty to the king and acknowledges membership of the Great Eastcheap society but offers no loyalty or commitment to God, the church, or the works of Swedenborg. He sees this as evidence of the "spurious and Babylonish" origin of the New Church (his position in the larger dispute about the origins of the church) and goes on to accuse Robert Hindmarsh of preferring secular to divine honor:

> Really, one cannot think of the preamble adopted by the members of the Eastcheap Society, and forget that Robert Hindmarsh was "Printer to his Royal Highness the Prince of Wales." Not that it is the desire of the writer of these words to set at naught human laws, and human honours, and governments, and dignities, far from it. Still he cannot feel unconscious of the force of the Divine interrogation, "How can ye believe, which receive honour one of another, and seek not the honour that (cometh) from God only?"[5]

Once again we see a sign of the larger dispute around church government to come. A request for the London society to give itself a formal constitution resulted in a statement that was largely a declaration of loyalty to the king. This intrusion of secular government into church government was a prominent feature of the argument at the conference the following year (see chapter 8).

The first two conferences were little more than a gathering of the London society with invitations to others to attend. They were dominated by the London members, notably Robert, who drafted and submitted most of the resolutions, and it was not until the third conference that the conference itself was asserting its authority and independence, notably in a resolution to develop rules of government and to take control of ordination. This lessening of Robert's ability to control the direction of the New Church may have played a role in the split that occurred after the fourth conference in 1792.

Meanwhile, in June 1791 a New Jerusalem temple was opened in Birmingham, with the first service attended by Robert and also Joseph

4. Anon., *Minutes of the First*, 68–69.

5. Robinson, *Remembrancer and Recorder*, 99–100.

Priestley, a prominent scientist, theologian and political thinker of the time. They were introduced and discussed the New Church doctrines, and Robert lent Priestley a number of books. Shortly afterwards, Priestley published a pamphlet, in the form of a series of letters, that was a strong and public attack on the New Church. Some of the key arguments Priestley makes are:

- The system of Swedenborg is new and extraordinary, and the more extraordinary it is the stronger the evidence required. Preceding dispensations were confirmed by miracles, and so surely this new one should be too. Swedenborg says he was not empowered because miracles compel belief and so take away the choice of whether to believe, but surely this was true of Moses and Jesus too.
- In the Bible God and Christ are always clearly spoken of as two distinct persons. And Jesus talks of having been sent from God and of praying to God. Was he praying to himself? As a Unitarian Priestley wonders why the New Church still clings to the idea of a Trinity, which is nowhere in the Bible; besides, the third part of their Trinity is not a thing but an action or operation.
- The idea of a purely spiritual second coming of Christ is inconsistent with Scripture, where it is clearly real and not figurative. It is contrary to the plain sense of Scripture.
- Swedenborg says God is love itself, is wisdom itself. This makes no sense. It is intelligible to say God is a being possessed of love, wisdom, etc., not that he is these things, except in a figurative sense.
- God having existed in human form from before the incarnation has no support in Scripture or reason.
- It is remarkable that Swedenborg provides no new information from the spiritual world—everything he saw was combinations of old ideas such as we see in dreams.[6]

The letters are all written in a friendly manner, beginning "my fellow Christians" and signing off "your friend and fellow Christian."

Robert was pressed by a meeting of the London society to write a response, which he did the following year, also in the form of a series of letters but in his case extending to nearly four hundred pages compared

6. Priestley, *Letters*. The points summarized here are from letters 2, 3, 5, 6, 6, and 8, respectively.

with Priestley's sixty-five.[7] Robert says that Priestley's arguments are essentially the same as those that others have made against Swedenborg and so he intends to answer all of them and thus ensure his work will serve as a response to other critics too. He also pledges to avoid any "unbecoming asperity" and maintains the cordial approach of Priestley. As an example of the nature of Robert's response, he argues that it is reason, not miracles, that leads him to conclude the truth of Swedenborg's works. Miracles were not performed by many great prophets—are we to deny the truth of Amos or Micah or John the Baptist? Miracles may also be the work of the devil, or they may simply lead to awe and astonishment and not the apprehension of truth, and so are far from an infallible guide to truth. Priestley said he would respond in turn but, despite a personal reminder from Robert, he never did.

Samuel Noble was in no doubt as to the effectiveness of Robert's reply to Priestley:

> Never was there witnessed in any discussion whatever, a more complete demolition of every one of an adversary's arguments, than was effected by Mr Hindmarsh for those of Dr Priestley.[8]

However, a correspondent calling himself Amicus was less impressed:

> I have read and perused your pompous and wicked advertisement, under the title *Letters to Dr Priestley*... this *Madman*, (namely Swedenborg,) and his foolish and vain Writings, are by you, and such wicked men as you, (for you should know better, and must know better, for your father was one of Mr Wesley's preachers; but I am afraid that worldly interest has led you aside,) setting opposition to the blessed Scripture. You would your vain and false philosophy, set up yourselves as men of consequence: but God knoweth, that real Christian experience, and the root of the *matter* is not in you. Against the glorious gospel of Jesus, you set up Swedenborg and yourselves; and under the cloak of opposing Dr Priestley, (who by the by is a far more excellent character, and more sensible man, than E Swedenborg was, or any of you are,) endeavour to introduce a *new gospel*. Eternal ruin and condemnation awaits you: you are now under the *curse* of God; and will be *damned*, unless you fly with broken heart unto the blessed Jesus, and receive pardon from God through his blood and righteousness: and if your heart

7. Hindmarsh, *Letters to Dr Priestley*.

8. Editors, "Rev Robert Hindmarsh," 405.

> is ever changed, you will retract your wicked writings, which are so repugnant to the holy gospel of my lord.[9]

One later writer (with no particular sympathy for Swedenborg) found wry amusement in the supporter of a visionary (i.e., Robert) using logic to refute a rationalist of the enlightenment but concluded it was remarkably successful:

> His "Letters to Dr Priestly" are written in the true spirit of the new church, and with very considerable ability. While he ingeniously repels the doctor's arguments, he openly asserts that socinians are not Christians, and that their grand peculiarity, the denial of the deity of Jesus Christ, is the unpardonable sin against the Holy Ghost. Were it not that the subject is too serious, involving the interests of eternity, nothing could be more amusing than this conflict between the opposing elements, fire and water, scepticism and mysticism. Nor can anyone who has been accustomed to regard the Swedenborgians as visionary enthusiasts, and their antagonist as an acute logician, fail of being surprised at the appearance of ease and success with which Mr. Hindmarsh combats Dr Priestley.[10]

Many years later Robert wrote a remarkable pamphlet called *The Interview Extraordinary: Or a Dialogue Between the Author and the Following Distinguished Characters, as Representatives of the Christian Church, so Called, Viz Athanasius, Arius, Socinus, and Dr Priestley*. It was written in reply to criticism of his *Seal on the Lips of Unitarians, Trinitarians, and All Others, Who Refuse to Acknowledge the Sole, Supreme, and Exclusive Divinity of Our Lord and Saviour Jesus Christ* and included with later printings of this book. It begins with the author, Robert, having a "transfiguration of mind"[11] in which three strangers, who turn out to be Athanasius, Arius and Socinus (all prominent figures in historical theological disputes about the nature of Jesus Christ), have come to find out who had dared to seal their lips. They begin by arguing among themselves, repeating some of the historical disputes, but then come together to ask Robert for the authority by which he silences them. Robert replies with a long speech, quoting extensively from Scripture, on the need to silence those who oppose the truth. All three agree that he has spoken well and acknowledge the worthiness of

9. Hindmarsh, *Rise and Progress*, 136.

10. Bogue and Bennett, *History of Dissenters*, 143–44.

11. Hindmarsh, *Seal on the Lips*, 4.

Swedenborg's followers. Then they bring up Robert's claim to have silenced Joseph Priestley, and Robert relates how Priestley had repeatedly urged him by letter to complete his reply to *Letters to Members of the New Jerusalem Church* so he could consider the arguments against him. However, despite having been presented with a copy of *Letters to Dr Priestley*, Priestley failed to provide any kind of response. After a year had passed, Robert and Francis Leicester went to visit him at the Unitarian chapel in London, where Priestley declared that, if his *Letters* should go to a second edition, then he would include a response to Robert, but this never happened. After this digression into an account of what happened in the relationship between Robert and Priestley, the imaginary narrative resumes and Priestley himself is summoned to the room to account for himself. Priestley confesses that he was thoroughly defeated in argument and indeed had been lucky to escape merely with his lips being sealed. Whereupon the four of them leave and the author returns to his natural state. The real Priestley, who had died in 1804, might of course have taken a different view.

8

Government and Politics

THE FOURTH GENERAL CONFERENCE in 1792 ended the peaceful atmosphere of the first three as a dispute over the ministry and church government, which had been brewing for some time, finally emerged into the open, with Robert once again being a key protagonist. Robert states that

> Hitherto the proceedings of the Church had been conducted with the greatest harmony, and unanimity of feeling and sentiment prevailed to an extraordinary degree. . . . This state of peace and Concorde, however, began to suffer some interruption in the present Conference, on account of a difference of opinion, which for the first time arose among the members, in respect to the appointment of Ministers in the New Church. This brought on an inquiry into the nature of the New Jerusalem doctrines, whether they were more favourable to an Episcopalian form of government, or to one similar to that adopted by Dissenters in general.[1]

The minutes of the third conference record that Samuel Hands's resolution regarding the place of the clergy in the New Church (i.e., on an equal footing with the laity) was agreed unanimously, and so it would appear that disagreement over this issue arose during the course of the intervening year. Boyle confirms that it was Robert who was the principal mover behind the dispute:

1. Hindmarsh, *Rise and Progress*, 140.

> The fact was, a few members of this conference, with Robert Hindmarsh at their head, endeavoured to induce their brethren to endorse a plan for an episcopal form of government in the New Church.[2]

The differences between the two sides of the argument were such that two sets of minutes of the fourth conference were eventually published. The majority edition, signed by twenty-five members of the conference, subsequently became part of the formal records of the New Church; the minority edition, signed by Robert, his father James, and five others, differs in a number of places. One of the most significant differences was that the majority minutes simply say that a resolution of the previous conference on the ordination of ministers ("in order to secure the harmony of the New Church at large, no person can in future be ordained a Minister, except he be first recommended by the Society to which he belongs, and the Approbation of the General Conference of the New Church be obtained for that purpose") was read and confirmed,[3] while the minority minutes include a long preamble:

> On reading the Minutes of the last Conference, article by article, objections were made, by several of the members present, against all those Parts which seemed to recommend the appointment of ministers in the New Church by popular elections. This brought on an inquiry into the nature of the New Jerusalem doctrines; whether they were more favourable to an episcopalian form of government, or to one similar to that adopted by the dissenters in general. Several of the members present, after much deliberation on the subject, gave it as their opinion, that, notwithstanding the universality of the doctrines of the New Church, which are capable of being embraced by men of all Denominations, and in some measure preserved in all the possible forms of church government, yet they are clearly and decidedly more congenial with the episcopalian Form, or that which admits of one visible official head, with a subordination of ministers under him, than with those of Presbyterians and dissenters, which admit of no single head, and in which there is no such subordination of ministers, but all things are determined by majorities. However, notwithstanding the many proofs which were brought from the writings of Emanuel Swedenborg in favour of the above sentiments, a considerable majority of the members of the present conference thought proper to adopt

2. Boyle, "Historic Notice," xxviii.

3. Anon., *Minutes of the First*, 78.

> that mode of church government, in which all questions are to be determined by the votes of the people at large.[4]

Another significant difference was that the minority minutes include a "declaration against infidelity and democracy," introduced by a speech from Robert, something entirely absent from the majority minutes. This declaration, Boyle tells us, was drawn up and signed by seven individuals on the day that it was produced and read to the conference by Robert. Its object, according to Boyle, was not so much a repudiation of the principles of infidelity and democracy but an assertion of Robert's doctrine of the priesthood.[5] However, this may be understating the significance of secular politics in the dispute. The minority minutes state,

> A conversation having taken place on the subject of ecclesiastical and civil government, Mr R Hindmarsh observed, that he thought it a duty incumbent on the members of the New Church, at the present critical moment, when the principles of infidelity and democracy were spreading abroad in the world, and threatening the peace of this nation in particular, to stand forward and declare their sentiments, in order as far as lies in their power to check the said principles of infidelity and democracy, to promote the interests of the true Christian religion, and to give satisfactory information to all persons inquiring into the real nature and tendency of the New Jerusalem doctrines.[6]

The declaration itself weaves together the principles of civil and ecclesiastical government, suggesting that Robert thought the two were closely related, as the following extracts illustrate:

> [We] therefore object against [republican or democratic principles] for the following reasons:
>
> 1 Because we believe and acknowledge, that all Power is derived from the Lord alone.
> 2 Because we believe, that all Ecclesiastical Power and Authority is delegated by the Lord to those whom he has been pleased to appoint to the Office of the Ministry, as Representatives of himself in Respect to the Administration of Divine Good and Truth in the Church. . . .

4. Anon., *Minutes of the First*, 142.
5. Boyle, "Historic Notice," xxix.
6. Anon., *Minutes of the First*, 145.

4 Because we believe, that those Ministers whom the Lord has appointed to the Office of the Ministry, and those Kings or Governors whom He has appointed for the government of Nations, are the proper mediums or channels by and through which the Lord appoints other Ministers and Kings or Governors.

5 Because we believe, that as all Kings and Ministers, in respect to their Office, represent the Lord, and not the People, therefore they ought to be appointed by the Lord whom they do represent and not by the people, whom they do not represent. . . .

13 Because we believe, that as a Minister is a Shepherd or Pastor, and the People the Sheep or Flock; and as the Sheep are entrusted to the Care of the Shepherd, by the Lord who is their Owner; it is an Absurdity to say, that the Sheep have the Right or Power of choosing and dismissing their Shepherd, and yet entrust themselves to his Care and Protection: for if they had the Power of displacing him, it is plain that they would be stronger than him; and if they are stronger than him, what Occasion can they have for his Protection? The Right and Power of protection against the Wolf would in such Case be in the Sheep themselves, and not in the Shepherd. But Sheep, as such, are helpless; and the Shepherd, as a Man, is able to protect them: Consequently the Shepherd has more Power and Authority than the Sheep, neither does he receive his Power and Authority from the Sheep, but rather communicates his Power and Protection to the Sheep.

14 Because we believe, that it is agreeable to Divine Order, and to the Writings of Emanuel Swedenborg, that there should be a Distinction of Ranks among Mankind: Whereas the Doctrines of Republicanism now circulating in the Country at large seem to confound all Ranks, and to place all Men on a Level, which we consider to be hostile to the Peace and Welfare of Society, both in a Religious and Civil Point of View.[7]

Robert later enlarged on the background to the views expressed in the declaration, again making it clear that he did not think the sole or main issue was the doctrine of the priesthood:

7. Anon., *Minutes of the First Seven*, 145–51.

> At the time when this conference met, the whole country, from one end to the other, was agitated by, contending political opinions, in consequence of the licentious and deistical principles, which followed in the train of the French Revolution, and which were then promulgated with much zeal on this side of the water, particularly by the democratical Mr Thomas Paine. By him it was urged, that the people at large had the undoubted right to call to account all who were in authority over them, whether in the Church or in the State, and, if necessary, to cashier and depose them at pleasure, not excepting the Chief Magistrate of the realm, even the King himself, who sat upon the throne. Many were the otherwise well-disposed individuals, in almost every class of society, who, taken as it were by surprise, and captivated by the artful and seductive reasonings of the above-mentioned writer, and others of the same stamp, too hastily and needlessly suffered themselves to be misled in their judgement, and to become discontented with the Constitution and Government of their country. It was to guard against the introduction of sentiments of this description, and to convince the world that the Writings of Swedenborg gave no countenance whatever to them, that a Protest was entered in the Minutes of this Conference against all such principles of infidelity and democracy as were then circulating in the country.[8]

The late eighteenth century was indeed a time of great political agitation. The fall of the Bastille in Paris had taken place a few months after the first General Conference, and Edmund Burke had engaged in public debate with Thomas Paine about the merits of the French Revolution. In 1791, the year before the declaration, Paine published the first part of *The Rights of Man*, which, despite being banned by the government, sold two hundred thousand copies in two years. And in Birmingham, riots had led to the destruction of many houses of those supporting the French Revolution, including that of Joseph Priestley. Groups of radical reformers, such as the various corresponding societies, were springing up all over the country and arguing for political rights. In response, the government became increasingly repressive, with the 1793 Aliens Act preventing French republicans from entering Britain, the suspension of habeas corpus in 1794, and the Seditious Meetings Act of 1795, which required any meeting of more than fifty people to be authorized by a magistrate.

Robert and his few supporters clearly viewed the desire for democratic church government as linked to the desire for democratic political

8. Hindmarsh, *Rise and Progress*, 142.

government, as the two are interwoven in the declaration. It is likely that they took the view that Swedenborg favored an episcopal form of government (or at least one in which ordained ministers took the primary role) and that any tendency towards a more democratic form was thus a pandering to democratic sentiments rather than a conclusion from Swedenborg. However, they may also have been partly motivated by fear of association with radicals and sought to distance the New Church from them. The Illuminati of Avignon, for example, had been blamed for the French Revolution, and so people with links to continental groups and ideas, such as Benedict Chastanier, could be regarded with suspicion. Similarly the secession of America had been blamed by many Anglicans on the plotting of English Dissenters, and there was a persistent sense that only membership of the Established Church was a sure guarantee of proper political behavior.

In considering these issues it is important to understand how key words were understood at the time, which is often quite different to how we understand them now. In particular, the word "democracy" had very different connotations in the late eighteenth century. The idea of democracy back then was largely discredited, being associated with ancient city-states and their rather tumultuous history. Anyone with a classical education would know that Plato had been highly critical of democracy due to the risk of tyrants and demagogues achieving power, advocating instead rule by philosopher kings drawn from the wise and virtuous. As the eighteenth century progressed, democracy became associated with the revolutions in America and France and was thought of as something closer to rebellion and anarchy than any modern notion of democracy. A loyalist "Creed of the Democrat" in the magazine *The World* began with "I believe in mobs . . . ."[9] The early parliamentary reformers wanted to extend the franchise but didn't see themselves as pursuing democracy, nor did they appeal to fundamental democratic principles. In contrast, Edmund Burke used the accusation of being democrats against the French Revolution, and Thomas Paine was denounced as a democrat in papers such as the *Morning Herald* and *The Times*.[10] The 1688 constitutional settlement in England, following the deposition of James II, had an important legacy here, as it introduced a mixed model of some democratic government alongside the aristocracy and monarchy. The pursuit of absolute democracy was seen as no more

9. Philp, "Talking About Democracy," 107.

10. For more detail about democracy in the eighteenth century, see Philp, "Talking About Democracy."

legitimate than the pursuit of absolute monarchy. Hence, to be opposed to democracy in the 1790s was simply to be conservative and loyal and was a widely held viewpoint.

Alongside this, radical Dissenters were seen as potentially subversive and dangerous. One writer put the Swedenborgians in such company and feared that

> the numberless multitude of Presbyterians, Independents, Anabaptists, Antinomians, Muggletonians, Swedenburgians [*sic*], New-Light-Men, Sandemanians, and the various motley description of modern Schismatics aided by the Turks and Infidels of all names and nations, with Lord George Gordon at their head and Jewish priests sounding the horns of sedition in his train.[11]

Lord Gordon was the Protestant instigator of the Gordon Riots in 1780 when, for several days, opponents of Catholic emancipation rioted and looted in London, including attacks on Newgate Prison and the Bank of England. These riots would have been fresh in the memory of many of those gathering in London for the fourth General Conference in 1792. Some supporters of Swedenborg even provided evidence for accusations of subversion. Benedict Chastanier quoted Thomas Paine in support of separation from the old church;[12] August Nordenskjöld wrote a pamphlet that was revolutionary in its implications (see chapter 2), and Wadström was frequently invited to the reformist Manchester Constitutional Society.[13]

In this atmosphere it is perhaps unsurprising that some early Swedenborgians wished to ensure that there was no possibility that accusations of subversion or disloyalty could be directed against them. We saw a suggestion of that at the previous year's conference when the London attendees were asked to constitute themselves formally and came back with what was essentially a declaration of loyalty. And Robert himself, though some distance in time later, said that the declaration was specifically designed to guard against the introduction of any discontent with the constitution and government of the country and that Swedenborg's writings gave no countenance to that whatever. The link was made again in an advert for Robert's *Letters to Dr Priestley*, which included the statement:

11. An Ecclesiastic [Rev Bradshaw], *Scourge*, 51.
12. Chastanier, "To the Editor," 359.
13. Rix, "William Blake."

> At a Time when the Principles of TRUE CHRISTIANITY, with their proper Effect SUBORDINATION in CIVIL SOCIETY, according to the Heavenly Form of MONARCHICAL GOVERNMENT, are just beginning to enlighten the World, and to be clearly and rationally understood, from the instructive Writings of the late Hon Emanuel Swedenborg; and when, on the other Hand, ARIANISM, SOCINIANISM, DEISM, MATERIALISM, and ATHEISM, with their necessary Offspring and Companion REPUBLICANISM, are making such rapid Strides over every Kingdom in Europe, but particularly in our own; it is certainly the Duty of every Well-Wisher to Religion, to his Country, and to Society, to assist in checking those Principles of INFIDELITY and DISCORD, which, from the Subtlety and Sweetness of the Poison they contain, the Ingenuity of the Arguments made use of to support and carry them, too easily recommend themselves to the unwary and simple-minded. To check, in some measure, the Progress of these alarming evils, the above Letters to Dr Priestley are written, and earnestly recommended to the Attention of the Public. In the Course of these Letters it is plainly, though briefly, demonstrated, that the Principles in which Mr Paine's *Rights of Man*, is founded, the *atheistical, dangerous*, and subversive of the true Order of Society; being addressed to the Weakness and Wickedness of human Nature, and flattering that Lust of Dominion in every Man, which ought rather to be subdued than encouraged.[14]

At around the same time Robert was offered the chance to print a pamphlet of the prophecies and revelations of Richard Brothers. Despite an offer to double or treble the payment, Robert declined, affirming his opposition to the more rebellious views around at the time:

> After examining the manuscript, and finding that it distinctly prophesied the death of the king, which I considered to be unlawful, and highly injurious to the welfare of society, I declined being a party in any respect to such an abuse of the liberty of the press.[15]

Robert was clearly very aware of the growing risks of being associated with sedition, and indeed Brothers was arrested for treason in 1795. He clearly wished to distance himself and the nascent Swedenborgian church from any revolutionary or democratic accusation. This was understandable in the context of a desire to establish a new dissenting church at a time

14. Anon., "This Day Were Published."

15. Hindmarsh, *Rise and Progress*, 122. Probably a wise decision, as Brothers was arrested for treason in 1795.

of an increasingly fearful and repressive government. As the *Declaration Against Infidelity and Democracy* shows, it is possible to make the argument that civil authority is vested in those whom the Lord has appointed to the kingly office while ecclesiastical authority is vested in those whom the Lord has appointed to ministerial office. Just as kings are appointed by the Lord, whom they represent, and are not elected by the people, so ministers are appointed by the Lord, whom they represent, and are not elected by the people. The effectiveness of this argument was partially dependent on an understanding of what ministers were, which brings us back to all the arguments over ordination. If ministers are called by God to a new and special status, then it makes sense that they should have the key role in church government. If, however, they are simply people with useful skills who can serve a congregation in a particular way, there is no reason why they should have any special position in the government of the church. The argument also depended on a view of monarchy as having divine sanction, even though it might be constrained by law as a result of the 1688 settlement.

Robert's approach to church government was not adopted by many of the other dissenting churches where authority was usually vested in individual congregations or assemblies of lay and ministerial representatives. When the Wesleyan Methodists tried to move towards authority being primarily vested in minsters, it led to (or at the very least contributed to) a number of splits, as the Methodist New Connexion and the Primitive Methodists begged to differ. And it was not an argument that commended itself to many of the Swedenborgians, as the dispute led to an immediate split in the Great Eastcheap society. Sibly attributed this to Robert's refusal to accept the decision of the conference and relates what happened:

> The immediate cause of the Society's leaving Great East Cheap was in consequence of Mr Robert Hindmarsh, who hitherto held the joint tenancy of the place [together with two others], having gone to the landlord, without the privity of Messrs John and Thomas Willdon, and induced the landlord to take him as the only tenant. Having so done, at the next monthly meeting for business, he came into the vestry and informed the meeting that he was now the alone holder of the place, and asked them what they could now do to prevent him from having the government of the Church carried on according to his own views; at the same time declaring himself not to be a member of the Society. The Society hereupon took umbrage and left the place.[16]

16. Sibly, "Address."

It was an extraordinary attempted coup, but it failed when the majority decided they would not be beholden to Robert's views on church government and left Robert with a church building but no congregation. Manoah Sibly had been away at the time for the opening of a new chapel in Birmingham and came back to find that all but seven of his congregation had found a chapel in Store Street, Tottenham Court Road, and would worship there if Sibly agreed to be their minister. He did and the majority went with him.

Even Odhner thought Robert had gone a bit far this time:

> Robert Hindmarsh himself appears to have been filled with disappointment and disgusted at the disorderly tendencies of his fellow members in the Church, and his impatience seems to have betrayed him into an action, which, if it has been correctly and impartially reported, was certainly hasty and inconsiderate.[17]

After the dispute about conjugial love, Robert was expelled, but he didn't leave the society—he carried on pretty much as though nothing had happened. This time, however, he did leave the society, which raises the question of why he did so over church government but not the authority of Swedenborg. Robert's detractors put it down to his arrogance, megalomania perhaps, and intolerance of other views. The attempted coup does suggest someone determined to get their own way by any means possible, though it should be noted that Robert, at the time, was not regarded as a minister and so would not personally benefit from the ecclesiastical government he proposed. There were probably also other factors at play that suggest a more complicated explanation. In the conjugial love dispute, Robert was aligned largely with the semi-detached radicals (Wadström, Nordenskjöld, et al.) and many of his closest allies and friends, including his own father, were on the other side. The social pull to remain within the majority group was therefore probably strong. In the church government dispute, however, Robert was on the same side as his father, and the others were people he was much closer to in background and outlook and so he would be much more comfortable with them in a group on their own. Alongside this, the dramatic seizure of the lease of the chapel created not only a financial issue for him (as sole owner of the lease) but also a public situation from which it would be hard to climb down without significant loss of face. Taken

17. Odhner, *Robert Hindmarsh*, 39.

together these factors made separation in the church government dispute much easier than in the earlier one over *Conjugial Love*.

Writing some forty years later, there is a hint that Robert realized that his actions may have been a mistake. He acknowledged that the majority might have been right at the time and that the presbyterian form of government, though imperfect, may have been preferable at that stage in the church's development, and that God's providence might have permitted it.

> What is best in theory, is often most difficult in practice; and that which in itself is most worthy of being countenanced and supported, may, under certain circumstances, be found altogether inexpedient. So in the present case the majority of the Conference may have acted wisely, as they certainly did sincerely, in the decision to which they found it their duty to come: and there is good reason to believe, that the Divine Providence, whose superintending care over the Church is unceasing, permitted a less perfect order to prevail for a season, until one more perfect could with safety be adopted.[18]

The following year, April 1793, there were two general conferences. The first, official, conference was in Birmingham and continued the series begun in 1789. It was mostly concerned with a series of propositions designed to "incorporate the members of the New Church into one regular and orderly society, in which concord and unanimity may universally prevail."[19] This included giving every society the right to choose its own minister and, if the society deemed their "moral character, cordial reception of the doctrines of the New Church and abilities as a teacher" appropriate, then this was sufficient qualification for their ordination.

A second conference was held at Great Eastcheap and consisted of what Odhner, with his usual bias, refers to as "seven of the most intelligent members of the Church in London,"[20] though Boyle tells us that there were only five.[21] They were essentially the remnants left behind when the majority decamped with Manoah Sibly. James Hindmarsh was elected president, with Robert as secretary. Most of the minutes, which ran to twenty pages,

18. Hindmarsh, *Rise and Progress*, 141–42.

19. Anon., *Minutes of the First*, 94.

20. Odhner, *Robert Hindmarsh*, 38.

21. Boyle, "Historic Notice," xxxiii. The difference from Odhner may have arisen if Odhner assumed that the attendees were the same seven who drew up the *Declaration Against Infidelity and Democracy* at the previous conference.

are taken up by a plan of ecclesiastical government written by Robert and presumably encapsulating his views on the manner in which the New Church should be run. It was very different to the propositions at the Birmingham conference and, among other things, defined three orders of ministry and divided the country into twenty-four districts: no one could fault the five attendees in their ambition for the future. The conference also suggested that any owner of a New Church temple, once indemnified of all expenses, should hand over the building to a trustee. To put this into effect, a document transferring the lease of the Great Eastcheap temple from Robert to be held in trust was included with the minutes. It is possible that Robert's seizing of the lease for Great Eastcheap was at least partly with the aim of putting into effect this civil aspect of his plan for church government. Robert makes no mention of the Birmingham Conference at all in his *Rise and Progress*.

Meanwhile, the Great Eastcheap society was very small after the secession of the majority with Manoah Sibly and left the Great Eastcheap chapel at the end of 1793 to meet in members' houses. This they did for several years until Richard Thompson and Ralph Hall built a chapel in Cross Street, Hatton Garden for them. Initially Robert was a partner with Hall and Thompson, but once the land had been purchased a plan was conceived for a much larger building at a cost of £3,000 instead of £1,000. Robert, who had just completed a new house and printing works in Old Bailey for himself, felt this was a financial commitment too far and relinquished his share in the building. Robert traveled to Birmingham and managed to persuade Joseph Proud to come to London to be the minister when the temple opened in 1797.[22]

The society started small but, under the influence of the preaching of Proud, it grew. After less than two years the proprietors of the chapel, seeing the increased congregations, asked for a substantial increase in the rent. Proud's view was that the proprietors thought the society would have no option but to pay a higher rent (and that making money had been their original motive in building the chapel). However, shortly after the request, and quite by chance, Proud was passing through York Street and noticed an empty chapel. He inquired and found that it was available, and the society readily agreed to move. Another factor in Proud's departure was a new liturgy, composed by Robert, that the proprietors wished to use. Proud wished to remove some of the distinctively Swedenborgian features of the

22. Proud, "Memoirs," 12–13.

liturgy so as to make it less unfamiliar and more acceptable to strangers, but this was not acceptable to the proprietors.

Thompson and Hall, faced with an empty chapel, offered Robert Hindmarsh £100 per year to be the minister.[23] He agreed, but had little success in the face of the competition from Sibly and Proud, both formidable preachers, and before long the chapel was closed.

23. Proud, "Memoirs," 16.

9

Stockbroking and Salford

As the New Church settled down and the series of conferences came to an end (after 1793 the next one would be 1807), fewer records of Robert's activity were generated. He remained part of the Cross Street, Hatton Garden society, but after it ceased to meet following the departure of Proud it is not clear where his allegiances lay. Meanwhile, in his secular life, Robert continued to publish extensively—at least forty-two major works in the period 1794–97—but around 1798 he closed his printing business and became a stockbroker. Robert makes no mention of this in *Rise and Progress* so it is only possible to speculate about what the reasons were for this change of career. It may have been that printing was becoming increasingly uneconomic (the wages of highly skilled compositors increased from c. £60 a year to c. £75 a year between 1792 and 1793[1]), but perhaps more significantly the economy was very volatile, with inflation at nearly 100 percent between 1790 and 1800 and very variable from year to year. Printing was also becoming a riskier profession as the government cracked down on opposition in the wake of the French Revolution and domestic unrest, so a combination of financial and personal risk might have provided a motivation for abandoning it.

A rather more unlikely suggestion comes as a result of Robert having been granted a patent in 1798, with a later commentator[2] suggesting that a search for capital for his invention might have led him towards

1. Bowley and Wood, "Statistics of Wages."

2. Anon., "Notes and Reviews," 364.

stockbroking. The patent, from a "Robert Hindmarsh of Walworth, in the County of Surrey, Printer," was for "a method of applying an elementary or physical power to blast furnaces, and for all other works where power is required."[3] It was essentially a device that, through a system of valves and cylinders, used hydraulics (i.e., water pressure) to power a machine. The first part describes using a fall of water to achieve this but then goes on to describe an extension whereby another piston lifts the water back up again, turning his hydraulic device into a putative perpetual motion machine. It might seem surprising for someone so well educated and intellectually curious to be advocating perpetual motion but this was before the development of modern thermodynamics and so its impossibility was less obvious at the time. The lack of records of any other plausible Robert Hindmarsh in London at that time and the description of him as a printer means that Robert and the author of the patent were almost certainly the same person. Walworth is only just over the river from Clerkenwell, and one of his sons lived there (in 1825 but probably earlier too), so a move there would be quite possible. Perhaps the scientific elements of his education and his occupation as a printer gave him sufficient knowledge of mechanical engineering for such a patent, but it is nonetheless a surprising departure from his other activities.

Another speculation was that Robert's move to stockbroking was an attempt to generate funds to put the New Church on a secure financial footing after his experience with the Great Eastcheap and Hatton Garden temples.[4] This is possible, but would be an odd choice to make given his success as a printer and the uncertainties of stockbroking unless there was some other motivation for the change. Also, the change of profession coincided with a diminished role within the New Church such that in 1805 there was an exchange of correspondence about whether he had renounced the New Church entirely:

> Has Robert Hindmarsh *totally* renounced? I cannot positively answer this question, though I apprehend he is in a very cold state, towards the northern quarter; his profession at present is that of a Stock Broker, and I have been told he had acquired considerable sums by speculating in the public funds. The

3. Anon., *Repertory*, 217.

4. Williams-Hogan, "New Church," 591.

> *amor sui mundique* [love of self and the world] seem to absorb his whole attention.[5]

The conclusion was that he had not left the church, but Servanté seems to be suggesting that he lost much of his former enthusiasm. Robert did not attend either of the conferences held in 1807 and 1808, and the *Faraday Index of New Church Periodicals* has nothing for Robert in this period, which was unusual for such a prolific writer. However, Robert had not completely lost interest in the New Church in this period, as in 1802,

> curiosity led me, as well as many other Englishmen, to visit Paris. Knowing that a small society of readers of the new doctrines existed in that city before the Revolution of 1789, I was desirous of ascertaining the state of that society, after the many convulsions which had taken place in the political world. On inquiry, I found the Society still met together occasionally, but not regularly; and on Sunday, Sept. 5th, I attended one of their meetings, which consisted of about twelve persons, who had been collected together by some of our English friends then in Paris.[6]

He was also unimpressed by "the total abstinence of all the public decencies of religion on the Sabbath day"[7] with shops remaining open, workmen at work, and washer-women washing.

Robert was a member of the London Stock Exchange from 1802 (the year after its formation) until 1809,[8] but he may have been an active trader for longer, as he described himself in 1807 as "ten years a member." He resigned from the Exchange in 1807, but his official connection remained until 1809, probably in order to discharge his obligations (considerable losses) at the time of his resignation. Robert had invested in a government lottery, something that had been a regular means of fundraising for the government throughout the eighteenth and early nineteenth centuries. In Robert's time the lottery was in essence a simple affair: people, often ordinary people, bought tickets (or shares of tickets) in the hope of receiving a cash prize, while the profits went to the treasury. However, around the lottery itself was a huge market in side bets on the outcome. The lottery

5. Servanté, "Epistolary Correspondence II," 312. "Northern quarter" may be a reference to Swedenborg's *Heaven and Hell*, where hell is divided into quarters and the northern quarter is for those, among others, who were in love with the world.

6. Hindmarsh, *Rise and Progress*, 181.

7. Hindmarsh, *Rise and Progress*, 182.

8. Anon., "Applications for Admission."

tickets were traded and usually increased in price as the draw approached. The draw took place over several days, and so ticket prices could be affected dramatically by whether any of the large prizes had been won on any given day. Tickets could even be hired for a specified length of time, giving a return if they were drawn during that period. However, by the early nineteenth century a new market in "produces" had developed, which was the difference between the contract price of the lottery ticket and the gain or loss relative to this, i.e., a bet on how much the ticket would change in price during the lottery. In itself this was not necessarily a problem, but the existence of a market in produces provided a strong incentive towards activity designed to manipulate the price of lottery tickets and hence the produces. In the case of the 1807 lottery, the managers of the lottery appear to have bought back three thousand of the twenty-five thousand tickets available, thereby reducing the supply of the tickets and driving up both the price of the tickets and the value of the produces.

It seems that Robert was a buyer and seller of produces and, along with many others, became a victim of this market manipulation, presumably because he was liable to pay out on the higher value of the produces. A number of those traders in produces complained to the stock exchange that the management of the lottery had been fraudulent and that therefore any payments on produces accounts were void. The stock exchange investigated (though not very thoroughly as it all took place on one day) and declared that the contracts were valid and should be paid. Robert considered refusing to do so until such time as the issue had been properly investigated and adjudicated on but decided instead to pay his debts and resign from the stock exchange. Of course, being Robert Hindmarsh, he didn't merely resign from the stock exchange; he made a speech to them denouncing the nefarious activities and then had the speech, together with an explanatory introduction, printed and circulated.

> Gentlemen, It is now ten years since I first became a member of the Stock Exchange during all which time, I trust, I have conducted myself in such a manner as to give entire satisfaction to every gentleman who has honoured me with his confidence, or with whom I have had any transactions whatever. I have hitherto always paid twenty shillings to the pound, yet not without great difficulty on some pressing occasions and up to the present day no man can claim a shilling of me although (as you may well suppose from your own individual experience) some thousands of pounds

> at this moment due to me, the whole of which I deem irrecoverably lost.
>
> I have good reason to believe . . . I should in reality be entitled to a clear profit of £1,000. Gentlemen, I do not pretend to be a rich man, neither do I complain of my poverty, I thank God however, that I am what I am and although I have within the last eighteen or twenty months, actually lost in this House upwards of £2,000 I am nevertheless still able to pay all my just debts and even those claims which in my heart I believe to be unjust.[9]

Manoah Sibly explains the losses of over £2,000 (some £150,000 in today's money) as being the result of Robert's lack of experience in the machinations of the world of finance:

> Prior to his going to Manchester, and being out of business, he engaged in a speculative occupation, not at all suited to his still and quiet genius: and being inexperienced in the artifices practised by those who are usually engaged in the line he was then pursuing, he found himself, after a time, to be a loser: I do not know to what amount: but to the honour of the church it may be mentioned, that although the losses were not legally binding on him, yet he paid the whole. He thus came out from among them with clean hands; and surely, I may say, with a pure heart: and he made the sacrifice, notwithstanding the voluntary payments, as they might be called, left him a poor man, in comparison with what his circumstances in life had been before.[10]

Once again we see Robert's high principles at work: despite having a possible legal way out, he considered it right to honor the debts despite a very substantial cost to himself. As Hyde commented, "The earnestness that was begotten at Kingswood, that was nurtured at Great Eastcheap, did not forsake him when he stood before his fellows in the Stock Exchange to say farewell."[11]

Having first abandoned printing and then the stock exchange, Robert, now in his early fifties, needed a new occupation and a source of income. At first he occupied himself with revised translations of two of Swedenborg's works that were published by the Printing Society of London in 1810. Then he was approached by William Cowherd, pastor of a New Church chapel in Peter Street, Manchester, to join him in publishing translations of

9. Hindmarsh, "Speech Delivered to Members."

10. Editors, "Rev Robert Hindmarsh," 412–13.

11. Hyde, "Some Notes II," 122.

Swedenborg's works. Thus in January 1811 he set out on the long journey from London to Manchester to start this new venture. However, the move proved to be a mistake: Cowherd was not really interested in publishing and merely wanted to lend the name of Robert Hindmarsh to his own activity.

> I at length, after some hesitation and reflection, accepted the invitation to remove to Manchester, where I arrived in January, 1811. But I had not been there long before I discovered, that Mr Cowherd was not the man I had charitably supposed him to be, notwithstanding the unfavourable reports, which had reached my ear. His eccentricity of character, joined to an overbearing and conceited opinion of his own transcendent abilities, which he blushed not to represent as far superior to those of every other reader of the Writings, soon convinced me, that the expectations I had entertained of the probable success of our joint efforts in the way contemplated, could never be realised. I had reason also to believe that my visit to him for the ostensible purpose of assisting in the translation of publication of the works before mentioned, was made a cloak to shelter a concealed design, which afterwards became manifest, of having it generally understood, that I had adopted his peculiar sentiments, and was come to support them against all opposition. Being satisfied, therefore, that my stay with him would be productive of no real good, and that the whims, to which he was constantly subject, especially those which regarded abstinence from animal food, and the use of fermented liquors, which he strenuously insisted upon as a religious duty, to be observed by all the members of the Church, I determined, after about three months trial of the spirit that harassed and worried him, to withdraw from all connection with him, and return to London.[12]

Goyder relates that the last straw for Robert was a berating that Cowherd gave to his wife, Sarah:

> Mr Cowherd having in vain endeavoured to draw over to his opinions Mr Hindmarsh now had recourse to another expedient. He paid a visit to Mrs Hindmarsh during her husband's absence, and after representing the great sin of eating flesh and drinking fermented liquors, concluded his exhortation by a furious philippic at the conduct of both herself and her husband, declaring that all eaters of flesh were gluttons, and all drinkers of fermented liquors were drunkards. On Mr Hindmarsh being acquainted with this unprovoked and cowardly attack, he immediately resolved to drop

12. Hindmarsh, *Rise and Progress*, 203–4.

> the connection, and accordingly he shortly after quitted Mr Cowherd's service.[13]

However, before he could return to London, Robert was prevailed upon to accept the position of pastor to a congregation in Salford. He was engaged at a salary of £100 per year (which was considerably less than he had been earning as a printer), and some rooms in Clarence Street[14] were converted for him.

A curious footnote to Robert's career dates from this time. Dean's *Manchester and Salford Directory* for 1813 includes in its listing of churches in Manchester and Salford an "Immanuelites Meeting, Princess Street: Rev R Hindmarsh."[15] This use of the term Immanuelites is almost unique in the history of the New Church. There is a rare Swedenborgian Bible dating from 1809 that describes itself as being "printed for the Society of Immanuelites"[16] and a prospectus for a new work by Robert to be entitled "Immanuel" and including a proposal to call the New Church by that name.[17] As far as can be determined the work was never written or published. Exactly what was happening here is obscure, but it may be that Robert, having spent time away from a leading role in the New Church, was contemplating a new version of the New Church with a new name. For whatever reason the idea seems to have been dropped, perhaps because the builders of the new chapel that was soon to be opened for him didn't like this new departure, but that is all speculation.

The rooms in Clarence Street proved to be in a poor position. Robert had some difficulty in attracting a congregation, and an attempt at a school of theology had to be abandoned because some people came to disrupt the meetings and publicly insult him. Goyder relates that several times Robert almost left to return to London:

> The congregation continuing very slender at the room in Clarence Street, it was contemplated to give up all hope of raising a society. Twice Mr Hindmarsh had his goods packed up and was on the point of departure for London, and twice was this room closed, and again opened to the public; his friends were exceedingly

13. Goyder, *Concise History*, 110.

14. Clarence Street is sometimes referred to as Princess Street—the rooms were probably at the junction between the two roads.

15. Anon., *Manchester and Salford Directory*.

16. Bentley, "Swedenborgian Bible," 64.

17. Schreck, "Immanuelites."

> reluctant to part with him, and on the evening preceding his intended departure, when he had not so much "as a candlestick unpacked", it was contended that the erection of a New Temple would be only means of raising a society, and of permanently establishing Mr Hindmarsh among them. The idea was no sooner presented than grasped, and Mr Hindmarsh had once more to unpack.[18]

Thus, two years after he was first engaged, a new chapel in Bolton Street, Salford, was built, with seating for 450 and a stove for the winter, at a cost of nearly £2,000 (c. £110,000 today).[19] Robert opened it on September 19, 1813 with "a discourse . . . [that] was at once judicious, edifying and impressive . . . and if any persons were induced to attend from motives of curiosity, I have no doubt whatsoever, that they retired both satisfied and improved."[20] A collection towards the cost amounted to £51 8s (about £3,500 today).

Goyder described his qualities as a preacher, giving him a somewhat mixed review:

> So far is Mr Hindmarsh from having studied preaching as an art that he has been heard to say it was what he abominated. His utterance is at once rapid and natural, flowing inconceivably easy, and productive of great effect upon such elevated minds as are capable of understanding him. He is so exceedingly well read in all the Writings of our author that his discourses appear as combining all the luminous views of Emanuel Swedenborg, whilst they are couched in language of the most elegant and dignified description. He is not very apt in Scriptural quotation, but his comparisons and illustrations are striking and beautiful in the extreme. For a congregation of old recipients of the New Church, I look upon him as being the Minister most likely to be useful, for it is no disparagement to other ministers to state that his knowledge of the Doctrines is superior to most, equal to all, and inferior to none. But where there is a society of new recipients, or where they are young men, I do not consider him as likely to be so eminently useful; still, in making this assertion, I wish it to be understood that the fault would be more in the hearer than in the speaker; his discourses being mostly of that interior and spiritual kind, only

18. Goyder, *Concise History*, 111.

19. Anon., *Description*.

20. FMH, "Opening," 46.

> fitted to those who have been long receivers and readers of the Writings.[21]

Odhner, as you might expect, did not entirely agree. After quoting Goyder he comments,

> No faithful preacher of the Internal Sense of the Word can wish for higher praise than this, but Mr Goyder is evidently mistaken in his estimate of Hindmarsh's power of accommodating his presentation of the Doctrines to the apprehension of the simple or uninstructed. Few, if any, of the ministers of the Church have enjoyed more signal success than did Hindmarsh in the work of external evangelization, whenever he applied himself to it.[22]

Bayley also praised his preaching and went on to extol his virtues in argument:

> A large and neat chapel was built for him in Salford; where the copious variety of brilliant truths which ever flowed with ready elocution from his tongue, speedily attracted many admirers, and drew together a considerable congregation. . . . He was also eminently qualified for usefulness as a teacher by his talents for conversation and oral discussion; in which few men were his equals. That rare trait in his character, should here be noticed to his praise; that no man knew how to press an argument more strongly or to detect more acutely the fallacies in the argument of his opponent, yet no warmth or rudeness of contradiction which he might experience could ever ruffle his temper, or turn him aside from the point in question, to retort reproaches on his antagonist.[23]

Notwithstanding the doubts about his suitability for preaching to the uninitiated, Robert undertook a number of preaching tours around the country. In 1816 he went to Essex and, because a particular vociferous opponent of the New Church was located there, decided to go to Colchester. He had permission to use the town hall, but this was revoked when local clergy and businessmen got nervous, so he was forced to find rooms in an inn close to the town. Just before the lecture was due to start, the landlord announced that he had been threatened with a fine if anything of a political nature was said. Robert assured him that the lecture would be purely

21. Goyder, *Concise History*, 112.
22. Odhner, *Robert Hindmarsh*, 47–48.
23. Bayley, *New Church Reader*, 199.

theological, and despite some Methodist preachers muttering dissent, the lecture went ahead.

In 1817 he went on a six-week tour of Scotland and the north of England, taking in Glasgow, Edinburgh, Newcastle, Hull, York, and Leeds. In a series of letters he reports preaching to crowds of several hundred (1,200 on one occasion) and that some even traveled from Glasgow to Edinburgh to hear him a second time. Traveling south from Edinburgh he visited Newcastle, York, and Hull before returning home to Salford. He must surely have passed through Alnwick on his journey, but unfortunately there is no record of him having stopped off to visit his relatives there.[24]

During his time in Salford, Robert published a number of books, including a 350 page defense of Swedenborg's doctrines, *A Seal upon the Lips of Unitarians, Trinitarians, and All Others Who Refuse to Acknowledge the Sole, Supreme, and Exclusive Divinity of Our Lord and Saviour Jesus Christ.* He was elected president of the eighth General Conference in 1815 and of all the conferences between 1818 and 1822. In 1820, J. G. Pike, a Baptist minister in Derby, published the critique of the New Church entitled *Swedenborgianism Depicted in Its True Colours* that we encountered in chapter 6. Robert's reply was published the following year as *A Vindication of the Character and Writings of the Honourable Emanuel Swedenborg, Against the Slanders and Misrepresentations of the Rev J G Pike* and, aside from his comments on Swedenborg's concept of conjugial love, included a reply to John Wesley's accusations that Swedenborg was a madman. Goyder described Robert's writing in glowing terms:

> As a controversial writer Mr Hindmarsh decidedly ranks the first in the New Church; his productions are at once fervid, bold, and animating: there is no dull prosing,—no affectation,—and though an excellent scholar, no far-fetched learning about him; then he enlivens his productions with so many sallies of wit and pleasantry, and masters his antagonist with such perfect good humour, that it is impossible not to be pleased with him. Besides this he never leaves his work half finished; as his numerous antagonists can sufficiently testify, nor does he either exhaust the patience of his readers by prolixity, or disappoint their expectations by too great brevity. In fine he is an able writer, and an unconquerable and accomplished defender of the New Jerusalem Church.[25]

24. Hindmarsh, "Missionary Proceedings."

25. Goyder, *Concise History*, 111–12.

In addition to his work with the church, Robert also showed his wider intellectual interests. He had already been a subscriber to books on a variety of subjects, including *The Whole Genuine and Complete Works of Flavius Josephus* (1792) and *Lectures on Natural and Experimental Philosophy* by George Adams (1794), suggesting he had read widely beyond Swedenborg and theology. In 1812 he responded to the distinguished astronomer William Herschel, who tried to argue that the sun was a habitable body.[26] Despite being a court astronomer, a knight, and a fellow of the Royal Society, Herschel was wrong and Robert was essentially right. In 1817 he wrote about the age of the earth, arguing that attempts to derive a chronology from the Bible were unreliable and citing evidence from the fossilization of ivory and the time taken for light to travel from the stars as evidence of a much older earth. He concludes:

> It is plain that no reliance whatever can be placed on the commonly received chronology of the Scriptures, particularly of the early books, which are now know to have been written for a purpose widely different from that of *mere history*: and therefore the real antiquity of the earth must be sought for in vain by those who expect to find it in the Sacred Code.[27]

Once again, Robert was broadly right at a time when his views were not yet widely accepted. Robert's depth of knowledge was also apparent in a lengthy discussion of the translation of a verse in Mark's Gospel[28] and, with references to the original Hebrew, in a discussion of the various words in the Bible ending in "el" (the word signifying God).[29] And in his "Observations on Astrology" he demonstrated that he didn't have much time for astrology, palmistry, or the transmigration of souls,[30] which was in keeping with his skepticism of the wilder millenarian ideas he encountered in the 1780s.

26. Hindmarsh, "Remarks on Dr Herschel's."
27. Hindmarsh, "Considerations on the Antiquity," 346.
28. Hindmarsh, "Remarks on a Supposed."
29. Hindmarsh, "On the Various Names."
30. Hindmarsh, "Observations on Astrology."

10

St. Peter's Field

MONDAY, AUGUST 16, 1819 was a glorious summer's day as Robert Hindmarsh walked the short distance from his home in Hodson Street, Salford, to St. Peter's Field, an open area in nearby Manchester.[1] He probably made his way across the River Irwell at the New Bailey bridge[2] and then down Deansgate to Peter Street, at the end of which was the open area of St. Peter's Field. He took the twenty-minute walk because he was interested to hear the views of some radical reformers, particularly Henry Hunt, who had planned a meeting there. They wanted fair representation in parliament (the entire county of Lancashire, which included both Manchester and Liverpool, had just two MPs at the time) and universal suffrage (at least for men—women would have to wait much longer). It was a popular cause: on the way to St. Peter's Field, Robert would have encountered countless other people going in the same direction and perhaps some local militia stationed in the nearby streets as a precaution. By the time he arrived at the Field around noon a large crowd, which would soon become some fifty to sixty thousand people, had already gathered there.

Robert saw the arrival of Henry Hunt on a carriage at around 1:40 p.m. and heard the huge cheer that greeted him. He saw nothing untoward or worrying, but the Manchester magistrates panicked at the size of the

1. A version of this chapter was originally published in the *Swedenborg Review*, 0.05, Winter 2024, as "Peterloo and the Politics of Robert Hindmarsh."

2. The Old Bridge at the top of Deansgate, nearest to his home, had been pulled down in 1817, and the new Blackfriars bridge wasn't completed until 1820.

crowd Hunt had attracted and ordered the militia to arrest the speakers and disperse the crowd. At this point Robert left, finding "it was necessary to provide for my own safety."[3] The result of the cavalry charges was at least fifteen dead and six hundred wounded and, with ironic reference to the Battle of Waterloo, the event became known as the Peterloo Massacre. Three days later Robert conducted the funeral for William Fildes, a two-year-old child knocked from his mother's arms by a cavalryman to become the first victim of the massacre. So not only did Robert witness the events that day, but he came into direct and personal contact with some of those who had suffered most.

At the subsequent trial of Henry Hunt[4] in York the following March, Robert was called as a defense witness and appeared on the ninth day of the ten-day trial. In response to questioning, he stated that he went to the meeting not to participate, but solely to observe. "I am not a radical reformer," he said, "I never associate with any party in the state. I do not consider myself a political character. In consequence of what I had heard of the radical reformers I went to the meeting to satisfy myself of their disposition, and of the state of society." He "traversed every part of the crowd to know the complexion of the meeting and did not remain stationed at any particular place." He saw "nothing in the character of the crowd that excited any fears in me for my personal safety."[5] In response to a question about the banners he had seen, he stated, "I consider 'Equal Representation or Death,' to be nearly the same as 'Liberty or Death'; I mean, that equal representation is essential to liberty." He was also asked whether banners stating "equal representation or death" or "let us die like men, and not be sold like slaves" indicated a safe meeting.[6] He would not be drawn, maintaining that the character of the meeting was wholly peaceful and that people had the right to give their opinion at a lawful meeting.

Two years later Thomas Redford, a hatter who had received a severe saber wound to the shoulder, brought a private prosecution against four members of the Manchester Yeomanry for unlawful cutting and wounding. The case was heard in April 1822 and Robert was again called as witness. He was asked about the demeanor of the crowd and testified that they

3. Anon., *Trial of Henry Hunt*, 264.

4. Anon., *Trial of Henry Hunt*. The trial was also reported in detail in *The Times*, with Robert's evidence appearing on March 28, 1820.

5. Anon., *Trial of Henry Hunt*, 264.

6. Anon., *Trial of Henry Hunt*, 265.

were "very peaceable; in a remarkable degree, peaceable and quiet"[7] and remained so up until they were dispersed. He said he saw no resistance from the crowd and did not see any sticks or stones or brickbats thrown at the cavalry.

The impression of Robert that emerges from these events is someone who was not actively involved in politics but who was nevertheless sympathetic to, or at the very least not opposed to, the ideas of reformers like Hunt. He agreed to be a witness for the defense in the trial of Hunt and for the prosecution in the case brought by Redford; he defended freedom of speech and the right of the protestors to assemble and declared that equal representation was essential to liberty. This is all rather different to the impression of his political sympathies we saw in the disputes at the conferences in the 1790s.

At the fourth General Conference in 1792 there was a major dispute about the appointment of ministers and the form of government of the nascent church (see chapter 8). Robert was a leader among those favoring the more episcopal approach and the dispute at the conference was so deep that eventually two versions of the minutes were produced. In the minority minutes, Robert made it clear that he thought the presbyterian view, as opposed to an episcopal view, was influenced by dangerous political developments of the time. He then read out the *Declaration Against Infidelity and Democracy*, which he almost certainly wrote himself, and which wove together principles of civil and ecclesiastical government. The declaration and other writings make it clear that he regarded the writings of radicals such as Thomas Paine, whose *Rights of Man* had been published the previous year, and the influence of the French Revolution as potentially leading to discontent with the government of the country and that he wished to "guard against the introduction of sentiments of this description, and to convince the world that the Writings of Swedenborg gave no countenance whatever to them."[8]

In all this Robert was taking an explicitly conservative stance, defending the monarchy and the current constitution of the country against the reformist ideas coming from the likes of Thomas Paine. This stance was probably at least partly a defensive one, as he states in *Rise and Progress*. Dissenters from the Church of England, such as Priestley, could be seen as potential rebels, and so it might well have been prudent for a new dissenting

7. Anon., *In the King's Bench*, 14.

8. Hindmarsh, *Rise and Progress*, 142.

organization to ensure that it was very clearly seen to be on the side of loyalty. There might also have been a personal aspect to this, as printers, Robert's own profession, were at risk of being accused of propagating anti-government material. These forces could have pushed Robert towards a more extreme loyalist, conservative position then he would otherwise have taken.

There is a hint that Robert's political views may have been more complex than simply siding with the conservative defenders of the status quo. In 1796 he voted in the general election (qualifying through his status as a Freeman of the City of London) and cast his two votes for the two Whig candidates.[9] The Whigs were one of the two main political factions in the eighteenth century (the other being the Tories) and, while their positions had shifted through the course of the century, they were more associated with the mercantile classes and city dwellers (as opposed to landowners) and Dissenters (as opposed to Anglicans); they were supporters of Parliament (as opposed to the monarchy) and reform of church and state. Thus Robert would naturally fit as a Whig supporter, though it doesn't necessarily mean he was a supporter of all of the aims of the Whigs.

Nevertheless, the contrast between 1792 and 1820 is striking. When Robert claimed at the trial of Henry Hunt that he "never associate[d] with any party in the state" this may have been technically true in the sense of not aligning with a specific political party (though he did vote for a particular party in 1796), but it certainly did not mean that he never took an explicitly political stance. He did in the 1790s, when he sided with conservatives and the monarchy, and again in the trial in 1820, when he declared, along with the radicals, that equal representation was essential to liberty.

Could it be that Robert remained a conservative and was merely being highly principled? He was not a man, particularly in those early years, to adopt cautious, subtle positions; he took on views and defended them fiercely. So his defense of free speech could have been a principled stand: he believed in the principle and was happy to defend it even when he had no sympathy for the views being expressed. However, the whole tenor of the reports of his words to the court is unlike the passionate denunciation of Thomas Paine in 1792; it does seem that he had moved with the times and become less conservative as he grew older. Or perhaps some less conservative inclinations, freed from the necessity of protecting a nascent New Church, had the opportunity to emerge more openly. The government

9. Anon., *Poll*.

might have been even more afraid of revolution than in the 1790s (the Peterloo Massacre led to the most oppressive legislation the country has ever seen), but Robert could see all around him, in the streets of Salford and Manchester and in his church in Salford, the growing effects of the industrial revolution. There was a poor and suffering working class and a rising and wealthy middle class, both excluded from social and political influence and pushing the country towards the Reform Act of 1832, which extended the vote to a wider range of (male) citizens. It seems that democracy was not quite such an anathema in his old age.

One of the other reformers and scheduled speakers to arrive at St. Peter's Field with Henry Hunt was Richard Carlile. He had only become a campaigner for reform a few years earlier, but by 1819 he was the publisher of numerous political works, including those of Thomas Paine, which he split up into pamphlets to make more affordable. In the chaos of the cavalry charges, Carlile managed to escape and, with the help of radical friends, made his way back to London. There he quickly wrote up an account of what had happened and published it in *Sherwin's Weekly Political Register.* The government responded by closing down the *Register*, but Carlile changed its name to the *Republican* and used the August 27 issue to demand that the murderers be brought to justice. For this he was arrested, found guilty of blasphemy and seditious libel, sentenced to three years in Dorchester Prison, and fined £1,500. On completion of his sentence he was rearrested for failure to pay the fine and sentenced to a further two years; the fact that he was now an avowed atheist probably didn't help. Meanwhile, the *Republican* was published by his wife until she was arrested, then his sister until she too was arrested, and then several of his shopworkers in turn.

It was while Carlile was in prison that he read some of Swedenborg's works and a pamphlet by John Clowes *On the Two Worlds, the Visible and Invisible.* He was sufficiently unimpressed to write, from his cell, a polemical response addressed to Robert because "I am informed, that you, are the person to whom Swedenborgians and others will look up for an answer to what I have to say."[10] He says that, of all the Christian sects he has encountered, the views of Swedenborg are the most preposterous and suggests that Swedenborg's spirit world existed only in his imagination. He concluded with a public challenge to Robert to defend any part of Christianity as a whole.

10. Carlile, "To the Reverend," 613.

Robert was reluctant to take up the challenge but after the urgings of many friends he decided to do so, publishing a pamphlet, *Christianity Against Deism, Materialism and Atheism*,[11] in February 1824 (which eventually ran to at least four editions). Not to be outdone, Carlile, presumably with plenty of time on his hands while in prison, responded in three further letters in the *Republican* in March 1824. The exchange was robust—the pamphleteers of the late eighteenth and early nineteenth centuries didn't usually hold back—though they both wished happiness and welfare on the other. However, they tended to argue past one another rather than with one another, as with many exchanges between theists and atheists. Carlile probably gets at the real difference between them when he claims to have rooted out all the prejudices and preconceived ideas he acquired from teachers and priests in his childhood.[12] He and Robert had such different starting points that it was always going to be difficult for them to address each others' position. No doubt Carlile's fellow atheists thought he did a splendid demolition of Swedenborg while Robert's friends thought he successfully repelled the attack.

11. Hindmarsh, *Christianity Against Deism*.

12. Carlile, "Serious Address," 395.

11

Resignation and Retirement

ROBERT RESIGNED AS PASTOR of the Salford society late in 1823. He had been reluctant to take on the role in the first place and in a letter to the trustees explains that he did not want to initiate his leaving but had been looking for a reason to do so. That reason came when the trustees decided to change the basis of his remuneration, making it more dependent on the receipts from the congregation and less on a fixed salary. He responded to the trustees:

> Undoubtedly you have a right to make such Resolutions as may seem expedient to you. But when these Resolutions are found to have a direct tendency to abridge the comforts, and to increase the cares, of a minister now far advanced in years, I should feel myself dishonoured and degraded, not only in my own estimation, but even in yours, as well as in that of the Society at large, were I now, after being so many years in the receipt of the present salary, to accede to such an arrangement, as that which has been proposed and resolved upon.
>
> Taking therefore into view these considerations, with others not necessary to be stated, I do hereby give you notice, that I intend to resign my situation as Minister of the Temple in Bolton Street, at Christmas next.[1]

The congregation tried hard to persuade him to stay, but he would not be moved:

1. Hindmarsh, "To the Trustees."

> In consequence of the receipt of your letter, and that my intention may not be misunderstood, I cannot help again repeating that declaration [i.e., in the letter to the Trustees, to resign], and frankly acknowledging, that my determination remains unaltered. It will, I can assure you, be a matter of deep regret to leave you as individuals, and as a society, from whom I have received many marks of respect and esteem, and with whom I have for a number of years cultivated the most sincere friendship. I trust, however, that no serious inconvenience will arise to the Society from my departure; and indeed I have no doubt that the Divine Providence will in due time raise up a successor, whose labours among you will be generally acceptable and perhaps more useful to the public, than mine have hitherto been.[2]

The tone of the two letters is strikingly different: To the trustees Robert is stiff and formal, opening with "Gentlemen" and signing off "your faithful and humble servant," reflecting his annoyance at the trustees' change to his employment. To the congregation, however, he is warm and friendly, commencing "Dear Friends" and signing "In the bonds of heavenly good and truth, most affectionately yours."

In April 1824 Robert was presented with a silver cup, inscribed "to the undaunted champion of the New Church as a grateful and affectionate tribute . . . for his valuable services during his ministry; and for his disinterested and unwearied zeal in the promulgation of the Heavenly Doctrines of the New Jerusalem for upwards of forty years."[3] He clearly believed that he deserved it:

> I have abundant reason to believe, that I was both loved and esteemed not only by every individual of the Society to which I particularly ministered, but by a wide circle of friends in the country surrounding the town of Manchester, to whom I paid occasional visits in the discharge of the duties of my official situation: and I am sure, that the affection manifested by all of them to me was on my part reciprocal, and equally sincere.[4]

Around the same time, Robert sat for a portrait by Joseph Allen, which Samuel Reynolds turned into an engraving. Reynolds was a very distinguished painter, having made portraits of Kings George III and George IV; many aristocrats, including the Duke and Duchess of Northumberland;

2. Hindmarsh, "To the Members."
3. Anon., "Testimony," 247.
4. Hindmarsh, *Rise and Progress*, 420.

and other distinguished people such as Humphry Davy, James Watt, and Edmund Burke. A copy of the engraving is in the National Portrait Gallery.

Robert and his wife now went to Canterbury to live with one of their daughters, but he spent at least some of his time in London. He continued to write books and articles, was twice more elected president of the General Conference (in 1827 and 1833), and traveled at least once to Manchester. In 1827 he attended the seventeenth anniversary meeting of the London Printing Society and gave a speech of "unusual eloquence, as if his very soul was speaking, for a considerable time, and the meeting was correspondingly affected. A more delightful [speech] was never witnessed."[5] In 1830 he wrote (in a letter declining an invitation to the anniversary of the Swedenborg Printing Society):

> Though I am an old member of the church, as well as an old inhabitant of this world, I yet feel the same youthful affection, for its truth and its propagation, as I did nearly fifty years ago.[6]

In the same year he resigned from the editorial board of the New Church journal *Intellectual Repository*.

Robert's son Charles died of consumption in August 1832, followed by his wife Sarah in 1833 after a long illness. According to Robert, she was, "a rare example of the affectionate attachment of a wife to her husband through life, and in the very article of death itself."[7] Robert returned to London from a trip to Manchester in February 1834 in very severe weather, contracting a cold from which he never fully recovered. In October 1834 he made a will, and in November he wrote, "My health has been extremely precarious for many months past, so that at times I despaired of ever completing the list [of errors in a printing of *Aracana Coelestia*]." He says, "even now I am very unwell, and write with difficulty,"[8] though the writing appears similar to a letter written in 1830 and isn't at all spidery. However, he could see the end of life was approaching and proceeded to settle his affairs and complete his *Rise and Progress*. In December he left London to stay with one of his daughters in Gravesend (though which daughter is not clear).

> The day but one before his death, he appeared to revive a little, sat up in the bed, and desired to have a particular volume handed

5. Anon., "17th Anniversary," 609.
6. Hindmarsh, "Letter to Thomas Shaw."
7. Hindmarsh, "Obituary [of Sarah Hindmarsh]."
8. Hindmarsh, "Letter to Dr Tafel."

> to him of his manuscript History of the New Church (a work on which, at intervals, he had been occupied for many years). He turned to a certain part, respecting which, it appears, the thought had struck him, that some alteration would be necessary. After examining it, however, for some time, he said it was all right, and that the work was quite ready for publication. With a mind thus perfectly at ease, he patiently awaited the hour of his release.[9]

He died at about 10:52 a.m. on Friday, January 2, 1835, at the age of seventy-six. He was buried nearby at Milton-next-Gravesend, and his friends and colleagues were generous in their tributes:

> In the manners of Mr Hindmarsh there was nothing of pharisaical austerity; his piety was equally free from the fanatic's gloom and the dissembler's affectation; and his equability of temper and cheerfulness of mind plainly evidenced that, in his estimation, religion was not intended to diminish, but rather to purify and exalt every human joy and pleasure, whether internal or external. In private conversation our friend was communicative, animated, and engaging; and here, as in his discourses from the pulpit, he was zealous alike to maintain the truth, and to expose the fallaciousness of error; his intelligent remarks, therefore, would sometimes appear sharp and indiscriminate, yet they were evidently made without any consciousness of improper feeling, and designed to promote the spiritual welfare of all with whom he conversed.[10]

> The Rev Robert Hindmarsh was the most distinguished of the ministers of the New Church. His courage and constancy; his earliest zeal for the advancement of true religion; and his peaceful end, were his striking characteristics, and bear a strong similitude to those of the prophet mentioned in the text. [2 Kings 2:12, "My Father, my Father, the chariot of Israel and the horsemen thereof."] Though the Lord alone is the essential defence and security of his church, still he provides for its prosperity, by raising up human instruments qualified to subserve its interests,—men whose understandings are enlightened by genuine truth, whose doctrines and instructions repel the attacks of open or insidious enemies, and who go forth in the Lord's confidence and strength, conquering, and to conquer . . . His time, his learning, his talents, his influence, and whatever he could secure from but scanty means of support, were all, for the protracted period of upwards of half a century, cheerfully devoted to the Lord's service. He maintained in all the

9. Noble, *Sermon*, 15.

10. Howarth, *Discourse*, 17–18.

> relations of life, as a husband, a father, a minister, and a friend, that uncompromising integrity, that devoted attention to duty, that ardent attachment, which, combined with true Christian piety and even child-like humility, commanded the universal affection and respect of all who had the high privilege of his association.[11]
>
> So long as the New Church exists, which will be as long as the earth endures, the great promoter of the establishment of the New Church distinct from the Old will be spoken of with honour; and the name of a Peter and a Paul will not be remembered longer than that of Robert Hindmarsh.[12]
>
> We truly behold the writer as riding on a white horse . . . grasping in his hand the bow of resistless doctrine, all the arrows darted from which are so many piercing truths or conclusive reasons, which hit with unerring certainty the exact point in question, and carry conviction respecting it,—and then going forth conquering, and to conquer.[13]

Death notices appeared in local papers across the country, including the *Perthshire Courier*, the *Salisbury and Winchester Journal* and the *Kentish Gazette*. In his will, his specific bequests included the silver cup presented by the Bolton Street society in Salford, a gold ring set with amethyst presented by the societies in Edinburgh and Glasgow, a picture of Swedenborg painted by his brother John, and Swedenborg's walking stick with the initials E. S. engraved on the top (now in the collections of the Swedenborg Society in London), all of which were left to his eldest son, Henry. A sword stick was left to his son George.

The fact that Robert owned a sword stick provides a sidelight on life in English cities in the late eighteenth and early nineteenth centuries. Up until 1829, policing in England was undertaken by unpaid parish constables, supplemented in London by the Bow Street Runners, a small group of detectives. With the population growth in London it was increasingly inefficient and ineffective, a situation that was only addressed in 1829 in London, with the foundation of the Metropolitan Police, and after 1835 elsewhere in England. So the city streets were not safe, and it is perhaps understandable that a relatively wealthy person might seek some form of protection when out and about. Indeed sword sticks were a fairly common defensive accessory for wealthier men at the time (there are records of Lord

11. The Editors, "Rev Robert Hindmarsh," 418.
12. The Editors, "Rev Robert Hindmarsh," 422.
13. Noble, *Sermon*, 11.

Byron, Robert Burns, and Thomas Gainsborough all owning one), as carrying a sword openly became less socially acceptable.

Later authors were not always so generous about Robert, as we have already seen in the comments on Robert's sectarian role (see chapter 4). One striking exchange came when William White published *Emanuel Swedenborg: His Life and Writings* in 1867:

> [Robert Hindmarsh] was a Cockney to the finger-tips—a Cockney in intelligence, impudence and ignorance. His portrait is an effigy of good-humoured impregnable conceit—of in short the founder "under the Divine Auspices of the Lord" of the New Jerusalem Church. Of reverence and ideality—the inmost and rarest of human feelings—he was nearly destitute. To him the New Jerusalem was no mystic city, but a sort of New Clerkenwell. It was a shop for the sale of theological notions warranted fresh from Heaven. With the contents of the ecclesiastical warehouse he was familiar from basement to ceiling. For rival establishments he had all the contempt of a crack salesman.[14]

Robert was not, of course, literally a Cockney, having been born in Alnwick and spent much of his childhood in Bristol, but it was perhaps a convenient misapprehension for White. He was the librarian and storekeeper to the Swedenborg Society in London, but he fell out with them spectacularly over the selling of spiritualist books alongside the works of Swedenborg in the society's shop. After failing to resolve the dispute, the society seized the premises along with a significant quantity of White's assets, only for White to seize them back with the assistance of two prize fighters and a number of their associates. The dispute was eventually resolved by the courts in the society's favor, but the result was that White's book, while a reasonably balanced assessment of Swedenborg, is scathing about many members of the New Church, including Robert, so it needs to be read in that light.[15]

A review of White's book in the *Intellectual Repository* gave a very different impression:

> We had the happiness of knowing the worthy Hindmarsh, the object of so much vituperation by Mr. White. His sincere and gentle character endeared him, both in London and in Salford, Manchester, to hundreds of men, who have been the very salt of the

14. White, *Swedenborg*, 612.

15. Lines, "Swedenborgianism and Pugilism."

> earth. It was unpleasant to him to be a leader, or even to preach, and he retired early from the pulpit, to the universal regret of his society, into comparative retirement at Gravesend. . . . We have heard these men tell of his single-mindedness and his virtues, with tears of tender affection; and while we know how usefully he lived, and how blessedly he died, we can but rise from Mr. White's bitter pages with pity for their author, and a hope that he may live to purify his volumes, from their acrimony.[16]

16. Anon., "Review: Emanuel Swedenborg," 178–79.

12

Who Was Robert Hindmarsh?

Robert Hindmarsh was not the pious saint who could do no wrong in Odhner's biography; nor was he the ambitious megalomaniac in the anonymous manuscript in the Swedenborg Society Library; nor yet was he the dissembling radical conservative implied by Schuchard's cover-up. These divergent views, particular when they appear among contemporary or near-contemporary writers, were often driven by differing assessments of the positions that Robert took on the various controversies that occupied the early years of the New Church. Those who agreed with him tended to be wholly positive, while those who disagreed could be quite caustic, perhaps reflecting the emotional intensity of those arguments. He was, though, a complex, many-sided character, and this perhaps opened the door to these diverse interpretations of his life.

Simon Schama described William Tyndale, the first translator of the Bible into English, as "an immediately recognisable historical type—austere, unswerving, a little fanatical, but tireless in the pursuit of his mission,"[1] and there is something of this in Robert too. Hyde similarly described Robert as "strong, assertive, and ardent," with a nature "such that he could not conceive another view than that he had himself taken."[2] When he applied this vigor and intellect to the defense of the New Church, such as in his *Letters to Dr Priestley* or *Vindication of the Character and Writings of Emanuel Swedenborg*, he was widely praised:

1. Schama, *History of Britain*, 284.
2. Hyde, "Some Notes II," 117.

> "[He had an] extraordinary talent as an expounder of the Sacred Writings, and for setting forth, in a clear and powerful manner, the doctrines of the New Church."[3]

> "[He was] one of the most powerful polemic writers."[4]

> "His productions are at once fervid, bold and animating; there is no dull prosing,—no affectation."[5]

However, when he applied the same talent within the New Church itself, he was much less successful and found himself continually consigned to a minority. He was one of a small group who urged the formation of a separate church; one of six expelled for their view of *Conjugial Love*; one of a small group who argued for an episcopal form of government at the fourth General Conference; one of five participants at the alternative fifth General Conference; one of a small group left behind by the departure of Manoah Sibly and the majority of the Great Eastcheap society; and one of a small group left behind by the departure of Joseph Proud and the majority of the Cross Street, Hatton Garden society. He was "zealous alike to maintain the truth, and to expose the fallaciousness of error," and "his intelligent remarks, therefore, would sometimes appear sharp and indiscriminate."[6] This perhaps points to why those around him, while admiring him in many ways, sometimes found it hard to follow where he sought to go.

Robert was a warrior for the New Church, and it was this imagery—Robert riding a white horse firing arrows of piercing truth—that Samuel Noble chose to use in his funeral sermon. This characteristic may have been valuable in driving the formation of the New Church as separate from the old, but proved a liability in the more delicate task of building an established organization.[7] Robert was not a charismatic leader who attracted followers; he was a forceful leader who provoked division.

Yet for all his ambition and assertiveness, Robert was not driven by personal aggrandizement. He was a leading force in the early New Church, something attested to by many contemporary writers, yet he often did this without holding formal office. He was the convener of the first conference and made the opening speech, but did not hold any formal position until the

3. Howarth, *Discourse*, 15.
4. Noble, *Sermon*, 10.
5. Goyder, *Concise History*, 111.
6. Howarth, *Discourse*, 17.
7. Williams-Hogan, "New Church," 588.

third conference, and then it was as secretary; he was not elected president until the eighth conference in 1815. In this he was completely different to John Wesley, a man who presided over and dominated eighteenth-century Methodism. Robert drew much from his Methodist background—a readiness to separate from the old church, a pragmatism in facing the problems of a new organization, and a desire for preachers (and later ordained ministers) to have the key role in running the church—but he had no desire to be a "King in Israel."[8] He did, however, want the New Church to be shaped according to his views and was prepared to take radical action to try and ensure that happened. His attempted coup at Great Eastcheap, the alternative minutes of the fourth conference, and the alternative fifth conference were all driven by his desire to impose a ministerial-dominated form of church government. Yet he was not a minister at the time and so would not have personally benefited from any ministerial power within such a structure.

He was also regarded with warmth and affection by his friends. His congregation in Salford were very reluctant to see him leave, and the sharpness of his argumentative discourse was much less evident in his personal relations:

> In private conversation our friend was communicative, animated and engaging . . . [and] his equability of temper and cheerfulness of mind, plainly evinced that, in his estimation, religion was not intended to diminish, but rather to purify and exalt, to fill and augment, every joy and human pleasure, whether internal or external.[9]

Another writer emphasized that he could be respected even if you disagreed with him:

> Mr Hindmarsh was as true a man as ever trod this godly earth. . . . I did not agree with all his opinions, but he was the last man to dictate, or trespass on another's freedom.[10]

There was clearly a softer side to his character that may have been less evident to those with whom he engaged in argument.

8. This was a phrase used by Methodists to indicate that they did not want another leader as dominant as Wesley had been. See, for example, Townsend et al., *New History*, 383–84.

9. Howarth, *Discourse*, 17–18.

10. Mason, "Letter," 188.

From the perspective of the twenty-first century, the conflicts and schisms in the early history of the New Jerusalem Church seem extraordinary. The passionate conviction and the vehemence with which religious views were expressed are rare in modern mainstream churches, but in their time they were perhaps less surprising and certainly not untypical of the Nonconformist churches. The Methodist Church also had its origins in the eighteenth century and saw a similar pattern of conflict and schism, with numerous branches splitting off from the parental Wesleyan Methodists. For example, the first Methodist church in Alnwick, Robert's place of birth, spawned two further chapels in the early nineteenth century, and many of the arguments in Methodism, as with the New Church, centered on the respective roles of ministers and laity.

Despite the efforts of Robert and others, the New Jerusalem Church never became a major force in British Christianity, and in many ways its center was never in London where Robert's founding activities took place. At the 1851 Ecclesiastical Census, the New Church had just fifty chapels and 7,082 attendees on the census date (compared with 229 Unitarian, 371 Quaker, and over eleven thousand Methodist chapels). Nearly half of the chapels were in the northwest (twenty-one, compared with three in London) where John Clowes had been one of the earliest readers of Swedenborg's writings. While Clowes never left the Church of England, many of those influenced by him did, including his curate Cowherd, whom Robert encountered in Manchester. A report of the seventy-sixth General Conference, one hundred years after the inaugural meeting at the London Coffee House in 1783, noted that there were sixty-three societies with 5,490 registered members.

Among the millenarians of the late eighteenth century, Swedenborg's followers were spared the disappointment of the new Jerusalem failing to arrive, as their millennium was spiritual rather than literal and had already happened, but they faced other difficulties. Bogue and Bennett suggested that the language used by the Swedenborgians and their approach to Scripture was problematic:

> They often hold language which sounds to ordinary mortals as incoherent raving, while the language of others presents to their minds ideas which were never intended to be conveyed. . . . To argue with them from Scripture is impossible; because they turn

> from the evident import of the words, to treat them as cyphers, of which only the visions of Swedenborg can furnish the key.[11]

Garret looked to a social explanation for their limited success, arguing that the New Church

> became a middle-class, protestant denomination lacking the social cachet and political influence of an established church, the traditions of puritan social and political consciousness of the Unitarians and Quakers, and the emotional vitality of the Methodists.[12]

Robert himself was undaunted by this modest success for his life's enthusiasm and labor. In old age he professed the same youthful enthusiasm for the New Church as he had had in the turbulent days of its origin.[13] He concluded his account of the *Rise and Progress of the New Jerusalem Church*:

> On taking a retrospective view of the proceedings of the Church in general . . . it is gratifying to be enabled to remark, that the exertions of those who have taken an active part in disseminating the knowledge of divine truth in this and other countries, has been eminently successful. Notwithstanding the many difficulties and prejudices, from which from time to time they have had to encounter . . . [they] have now the happiness of seeing the New Church established upon a secure and permanent basis. As citizens of the New Jerusalem, we are all embarked in the same glorious cause; and there is great reason to hope and believe, that the Divine Favour . . . will continue to guide her with its superintending care, and at length cause her to become a blessing to all nations, and literally, as the prophet says, "a praise in the earth."[14]

11. Bogue and Bennett, *History of Dissenters*, 138.
12. Garrett, "Swedenborg," 81.
13. Hindmarsh, "Letter to Thomas Shaw."
14. Hindmarsh, *Rise and Progress*, 504.

Bibliography

Abbott, Robert. "Establishment of the New Church as a Distinct Community." *New Church Magazine* 2 (1883) 145–55.

Anonymous. "The 17th Anniversary Meeting of the London Printing Society." *Intellectual Repository for the New Church* 15 (1827) 608–9.

———. "Annals of the New Church." *New Jerusalem Magazine* 4 (1790) 174–78.

———. "Applications for Admission to Membership of the London Stock Exchange." London Archives, UK.

———. "Baron Swedenborg." *Universal Daily Register* (London), Feb. 26, 1787.

———. *A Description of the New Jerusalem Temple in Bolton Street.* Manchester: C. H. Cowdroy, 1813.

———. "Great East Cheap Society Minute Book, 7 May 1789–7 Nov 1791." Collateral Collection. Swedenborg Society Library, London.

———. *In the King's Bench, Between T Redford, Plaintiff, and HH Birley, Etc Report of the Proceedings on the Trial of the Cause at Lancaster.* Manchester: C. Wheeler & Son, 1823.

———. *The Kramph Will Case.* Bryn Athyn, PA: Academy of the New Church, 1910.

———. *Manchester and Salford Directory.* Manchester: R. & W. Dean, 1813.

———. *Minutes of the Eleventh General Conference of the New Church.* London: T. Goyder, 1818.

———. *Minutes of the First Seven Sessions of the General Conference of the New Church.* London: James Spiers, 1885.

———. "Notes and Reviews." *New Church Life* 29 (1909) 358–65.

———. *The Poll for Members to Serve in Parliament for the City of London, 1796.* London: John Rider, 1796.

———. *The Pre-Existence of Souls and Universal Restitution Considered as Scriptural Doctrines Extracted from the Minutes and Correspondence of Burnham Society, in the County of Somerset.* Taunton, UK: T. Norris, 1798.

———. "Proposals for Printing by Subscription Emanuel Swedenborg's Spiritual Diary, by a Society of Gentlemen." 1791. Archives. Swedenborg Society Library, London.

———. "Remark of the Editors on the Above Paper." *New Magazine of Knowledge Concerning Heaven and Hell*, Nov. 1790, 404–6.

———. *Repertory of Arts and Manufactures.* Vol. 12. London: John Nichols, 1800.

———. "Review: A Remembrancer and Recorder of Facts and Documents Illustrative of the Genius of the New Jerusalem Dispensation." *Monthly Observer and New Church Record* 6 (1862) 128–34.

———. "Review: Emanuel Swedenborg: His Life and Writings by William White." *Intellectual Repository for the New Church* 14 (1867) 161–81.

———. "R Hindmarsh and the First Ordination in the New Church." Undated notebook. Archives. Swedenborg Society Library, London.

———. "Testimony of Respect to Mr. Hindmarsh." *Intellectual Repository for the New Church* 4 (1824) 246–47.

———. "This Day Were Published." *Lloyd's Evening Post and British Chronicle* (London), Dec. 10, 1792.

———. "To Hindmarsh's Creditors." *Caledonian Mercury* (Edinburgh), Nov. 7, 1799.

———. *The Trial of Henry Hunt*. London: T. Dolby, 1820.

———. "The Universal London Society for the Promotion of the New Jerusalem Church." 1789. Archives. Swedenborg Society Library, London.

Barrett, B. F. *Catholicity of the New Church; and Uncatholicity of New-Churchmen*. New York: Mason Brothers, 1863.

Bateman, Henry. "Letter from Dr Bateman." *New Church Repository and Monthly Review* 6 (1853) 144–46.

Bayley, Cornelius. *A Short Account of the Death of Elizabeth Hindmarsh*. London: R. Hawes, 1777.

Bayley, Jonathan, ed. *The New Church Reader and Class Book*. London: James Hodson, 1846.

Bentley, G. E., Jr. "A Swedenborgian Bible." *Blake: An Illustrated Quarterly* 24 (1990) 63–64.

Bernet, Roger. "To the Editors." *Aurora* 1 (1799) 235–36.

Body, A. H. *John Wesley and Education*. London: Epworth, 1936.

Bogue, David, and James Bennett. *History of Dissenters from the Revolution in 1688 to the Year 1808*. Vol. 4. London: printed for the authors, 1812.

Bowley, A. L., and George Hy Wood. "The Statistics of Wages in the United Kingdom During the Last Hundred Years. (Part V) Printers." *Journal of the Royal Statistical Society* 62 (1899) 708–15.

Boyle, J. R. "Historic Notice of the Early Conferences." In *Minutes of the First Seven Sessions of the General Conference of the New Church*, ix–xl. London: Spiers, 1885.

Carlile, Richard. "A Serious Address to Mr. Hindmarsh." *Republican* 9 (1824) 395–98.

———. "To the Reverend Robert Hindmarsh, Priest of the Sect of Swedenborgians, Officiating at the New Jerusalem Temple, Salford, Manchester." *Republican* 8 (1823) 609–25.

Chastanier, Benedict. "To the Editor." *New Magazine of Knowledge Concerning Heaven and Hell* 2 (1791) 358–60.

———. *Word of Advice to a Benighted World*. London, 1795.

Church of England. *Book of Common Prayer*. Cambridge: John Baskerville, 1762.

Clowes, John. *A Letter to the Rev J Proud in Reply to His Remarks on Separation from the Old Church*. Manchester: J. Gleave, 1818.

Collins, Paul M. *The Trinity: A Guide for the Perplexed*. London: Continuum, 2008.

Cooper, Thomas. "Memoir of the Late Reverend Thomas Cooper; Written by Himself." *Wesleyan Methodist Magazine* 14 (1835) 81–92.

Danilewicz, M. L. "'The King of the New Israel': Thaddeus Grabianka (1740–1807)." *Oxford Slavonic Papers* 1 (1968) 49–73.

Deck, Raymond H. "Blake and Swedenborg." PhD diss., Brandeis University, 1978.

Delta. "On the Use of the Lot: In Reference to the Origin of the New Church." *New Church Repository and Monthly Review* 4 (1851) 533–53.

Dobbs, Francis. *A Concise View from History and Prophecy of the Great Predictions in the Sacred Writings*. Dublin: J. Jones, 1800.

An Ecclesiastic [Rev. Bradshaw]. *A Scourge for the Dissenters; or, Non-Conformity Unmasked*. London: J. Parsons, 1790.

The Editors. "The Rev Robert Hindmarsh." *Intellectual Repository for the New Church* 32 (1835) 397–422.

Firmitas. "On Ordination." *Intellectual Repository for the New Church* 10 (1814) 92–96.

FMH. "Opening of a New Temple at Salford, Manchester." *Intellectual Repository for the New Church* 2 (1814) 46–48.

Fonerden, Adam, and John Hargrove. "A Valedictory Address to the People Called Methodists." *Aurora* 1 (n.d.) 6–8.

Garrett, Clarke. *Respectable Folly: Millenarians and the French Revolution in France and England*. Baltimore: Johns Hopkins University Press, 1975.

———. "Swedenborg and the Mystical Enlightenment in Late Eighteenth-Century England." *Journal of the History of Ideas* 45 (1984) 67–81.

Gibson, William, and Joanne Begiato. *Sex and the Church in the Long Eighteenth Century: Religion, Enlightenment and the Sexual Revolution*. London: I. B. Tauris, 2017.

Gordon, Alexander. "Hindmarsh, Robert 1759–1835." In *Dictionary of National Biography* 27. London: Smith, Elder, 1891.

Goyder, D. G. *A Concise History of the New Jerusalem Church*. London: Thomas Goyder, 1827.

Hernlund, Patricia. "William Strahan's Ledgers, II: Charges for Papers, 1738–1785." *Studies in Bibliography* 22 (1969) 179–95.

Higham, Charles. "A London New Church Advertisement." *Morning Light* 36 (1913) 516–17.

Hindmarsh, Andrew. *A History of the Hindmarshes in 15 Objects*. Sheffield: A. M. Hindmarsh, 2022.

Hindmarsh, Robert. *Christianity Against Deism, Materialism and Atheism Occasioned by a Letter Addressed to the Author by Robert Carlile*. Manchester: Henry Smith, 1824.

———. "Considerations on the Antiquity of the Earth and the Heavens." *Intellectual Repository for the New Church* 21 (1817) 345–52.

———. "Death of Mr James Hindmarsh." *Intellectual Repository for the New Church* 1 (1812) 220–21.

———. "Letter of Rev R Hindmarsh to Rev J Hargrove, 10 January 1817." *New Jerusalem Magazine* 15 (1841) 102–4.

———. "Letter to Dr Tafel, Tubingen, Germany." Nov. 1, 1834. Archives. Swedenborg Society Library, London.

———. "Letter to Thomas Shaw." June 18, 1830. Archives. Swedenborg Society Library, London.

———. *Letters to Dr Priestley*. London: R. Hindmarsh, 1792.

———. "Missionary Proceedings." *Intellectual Repository for the New Church* 24 (1817) 499–505.

———. "Obituary [of Charles Hindmarsh]." *Intellectual Repository for the New Church* 18 (1832) 290.

———. "Obituary [of Sarah Hindmarsh]." *Intellectual Repository for the New Church* 20 (1833) 437–38.

———. "Observations on Astrology, the Science of Palmistry, and the Transmigration of Souls." *Intellectual Repository for the New Church* 29 (1819) 305–14.

———. "On the Various Names in the Word Terminating with El, Which in the Hebrew Language Signifies God." *Intellectual Repository for the New Church* 45 (1824) 290–94.

———. "Remarks on a Supposed Error in the Translation of Mark 3:21." *Intellectual Repository for the New Church* 29 (1819) 281–88.

———. "Remarks on Dr Herschel's Hypothesis of the Sun's Being a Habitable Body." *Intellectual Repository for the New Church* 1 (1812) 137–38.

———. *Rise and Progress of the New Jerusalem Church*. London: Hodson, 1861.

———. *A Seal upon the Lips of Unitarians, Trinitarians, and All Others Who Refuse to Acknowledge the Sole, Supreme, and Exclusive Divinity of Our Lord and Saviour Jesus Christ*. Manchester: F. Davis, 1814.

———. "A Speech Delivered to Members of the Stock Exchange on Saturday March 28 1807, Occasioned by Certain Fraudulent Transactions Supposed to Have Taken Place, Relative to the Late Lottery Which Finished Drawing Feb 14 1807." 1807. Archives. Swedenborg Society Library, London.

———. "To the Members of the Congregation Meeting in the New Jerusalem Temple, Bolton Street, Salford." Feb. 17, 1824. Archives. Swedenborg Society Library, London.

———. "To the Trustees of the Temple in Bolton Street, Salford." Nov. 5, 1823. Archives. Swedenborg Society Library, London.

———. *A Vindication of the Character and Writings of the Honourable Emanuel Swedenborg, Against the Slanders and Misrepresentations of the Rev J G Pike*. Manchester: H & R Smith, 1821.

Horwood, Richard. *Plan of the Cities of London and Westminster, the Borough of Southwark and Parts Adjoining, Shewing Every House*. London: 1792–99. Romantic London. https://www.romanticlondon.org/explore-horwoods-plan.

Howarth, D. *A Discourse on Occasion of the Removal into the Eternal World of the Rev Robert Hindmarsh; with Some Remarks Respecting His Life and Character*. Manchester: T. Sowler, 1835.

Hyde, James. "Benedict Chastanier and the Illuminati of Avignon." *New Church Review* 14 (1907) 181–205.

———. "Some Notes Respecting Robert Hindmarsh: With a Critique I." *New Church Magazine* 24 (1905) 65–72.

———. "Some Notes Respecting Robert Hindmarsh: With a Critique II." *New Church Magazine* 24 (1905) 114–23.

Investigator. "On Ordination." *Intellectual Repository for the New Church* 2 (1814) 88–92.

Ives, A. G. *Kingswood School in Wesley's Day and Since*. London: Epworth, 1970.

JMH. "Methodism in Kent." *Wesleyan Methodist Magazine* 103 (1880) 581–90.

Layman, A. "A Letter Containing a Few Plain Observations, Addressed to the Unbiased Members of the New Church, Especially in London." 1807. Collateral Collection. Swedenborg Society Library, London.

Lehner, U. L. "The Trinity in the Early Modern Era (*c*.1550–1770)." In *The Oxford Handbook of the Trinity* 240–53. Oxford: Oxford University Press, 2011.

Lindert, Peter H., and Jeffrey G. Williamson. "Revising England's Social Tables 1688–1812." *Explorations in Economic History* 19 (1982) 385–408.

Lineham, P. J. "The Origins of the New Jerusalem Church in the 1780s." *Bulletin of the John Rylands Library of Manchester University* 70 (1988) 109–22.

———. "Hindmarsh, Robert (1759–1835)." Oxford Dictionary of National Biography. Sept. 23, 2004. https://doi.org/10.1093/ref:odnb/13348.

Lines, Richard. "Swedenborgianism and Pugilism: The William White Affair." Paper presented at Bloomsbury Project Conference, London, 2011. www.ucl.ac.uk/bloomsbury project/articles/events/conference2011/lines.pdf.

Lucci, Diego. "Reassessing the Crisis of the Trinity in Early Modern England." *Cromohs* 19 (2014) 153–64. https://doi.org/10.13128/Cromohs-15388.

Mason, William. "Letter from WM Mason." *New Church Repository and Monthly Review* 5 (1852) 187–92.

———. "Origin of the New Church Ministry." *New Church Repository and Monthly Review* 6 (1853) 41–45.

Moxon, Joseph. *Mechanik Exercises or the Doctrine of Handy-Works Applied to the Art of Printing*. London: printed by the author, 1683.

Noble, Samuel. *A Case of Entrance into the New Jerusalem*. London: James Hodson, 1838.

———. *A Sermon Occasioned by the Removal into Eternity of the Rev Robert Hindmarsh*. London: J. S. Hodson, 1835.

Nordenskjöld, Augustus. "Församlings Formen Uti Det Nya Jerusalem." Royal Library, Stockholm.

Nordenskjöld, C. F. "CF Nordenskjöld to CB Wadström." Jan. 31, 1784. Academic Collection of Swedenborg Documents 1664.31. Academy of the New Church Archives, Bryn Athyn College.

Odhner, Carl Th. *Robert Hindmarsh: A Biography*. Philadelphia: Academy Book Room, 1895.

Paley, M. "'A New Heaven Begun': William Blake and Swedenborgianism." *Blake: An Illustrated Quarterly* 12 (1979) 64–90.

Philp, Mark. "Talking About Democracy: Britain in the 1790s." In *Re-Imagining Democracy in the Age of Revolutions: America, France, Britain, Ireland 1750–1850*, edited by Joanna Innes and Mark Philp, 101–13. Oxford: Oxford University Press, 2013.

Pike, J. G. *Swedenborgianism Depicted in Its True Colours*. Derby, UK: Henry Mozley, 1820.

Pinks, Henry. *History of Clerkenwell*. London: Charles Herbert, 1881.

Priestley, Joseph. *Letters to Members of the New Jerusalem Church*. Birmingham, UK: J. Thompson, 1791.

Proud, Joseph. "Memoirs of the Rev Joseph Proud." 1822. Typescript copy. Archives. Swedenborg Society Library, London.

Rack, Henry. "Evangelical Endings: Death-Beds in Evangelical Biography." *Bulletin of the John Rylands Library of Manchester University* 74 (1992) 39–56.

Rich, Elihu. "Early History of the New Church." *New Church Repository and Monthly Review* 6 (1853) 540–49.

Rix, Robert. "William Blake and the Radical Swedenborgians." Mar. 20, 2016. https://thehumandivine.org/2016/03/20/william-blake-and-the-radical-swedenborgians-by-robert-rix/.

Robinson, T. *A Remembrancer and Recorder of Facts and Documents Illustrative of the Genius of the New Jerusalem Dispensation*. Manchester: Thomas Robinson, 1862.

Rowell, Geoffrey. "A Note on the History and Doctrine of the Burnham Society." *Proceedings of the Wesley Historical Society* 37 (1969) 10–16.

Schama, Simon. *A History of Britain*. Vol. 1. London: BBC Worldwide, 2000.

Schreck, E. J. E. "Immanuelites." *New Church Life* (1924) 247–49.

Schuchard, Marsha Keith. "The Secret Masonic History of Blake's Swedenborg Society." *Blake: An Illustrated Quarterly* 26 (1992) 40–50.

Servanté, Henry. "Epistolary Correspondence of the Earlier Members of the Church, Letter II." *Monthly Observer and New Church Record* 1 (1857) 311–15.

———. "Epistolary Correspondence of the Earlier Members of the Church, Letter III." *Monthly Observer and New Church Record* 1 (1857) 417–23.

———. "Epistolary Correspondence of the Earlier Members of the Church, Letter IV." *Monthly Observer and New Church Record* 2 (1858) 278–81.

Sibly, Manoah. "An Address to the Society of the New Church Meeting in Friar Street, near Ludgate Hill, London." 1839. Collateral Collection. Swedenborg Society Library, London.

———. "Obituary [of Isaac Hawkins]." *Intellectual Repository for the New Church* 33 (1820) 265–68.

Sigstedt, C. O. *The Swedenborg Epic*. London: Swedenborg Society, 1981.

Southey, Robert. *The Life of Wesley and Rise and Progress of Methodism*. Vol. 2. London: Longman, Hurst, Reese, Orme, and Brown, 1820.

Stanley, Jacob. "Memoir of Mr Edward Stanley." *Wesleyan Methodist Magazine* 5 (1826) 793–809.

Swedenborg, Emanuel. *The Delights of Wisdom Concerning Conjugial Love: After Which Follow Pleasures of Insanity Concerning Scortatory Love*. London: R. Hindmarsh, 1794.

———. *True Christian Religion*. Vol. 3. Chester: C. W. Leadbeater, 1797.

Tafel, Emanuel. "Early History of the New Church." *New Jerusalem Magazine* 33 (1861) 541–48.

Tafel, R. L., ed. *Documents Concerning the Life and Character of Emanuel Swedenborg*. Vol. 2. London: Swedenborg Society, 1877.

Tate, G. *The History of the Borough, Castle and Barony of Alnwick*. Vol. 2. Alnwick, UK: Henry Hunter Blair, 1866.

Three Old Boys. *The History of Kingswood School*. London: Charles H. Kelly, 1898.

Townsend, W. J., et al. *A New History of Methodism*. London: Hodder and Stoughton, 1909.

Vickers, John A. *Thomas Coke: Apostle of Methodism*. London: Epworth, 1969.

Wainscot, A. Stanley. "Interesting Historical Document." *New Church Life* 88 (1968) 463.

Wakefield, Roger. *Wakefield's Merchant and Tradesman's General Directory for London, Westminster, Borough of Southwark* [. . .]. London: T. Davison, 1794.

Ward, W. R. "Swedenborgianism: Heresy, Schism or Religious Protest." In *Schism, Heresy and Religious Protest*, edited by D. Baker, 303–9. Cambridge: Cambridge University Press, 1972.

Warren, Samuel. "Rev Robert Hindmarsh Vindicated." *New Church Repository and Monthly Review* 6 (1853) 143–44.

Watmough, A. *A History of Methodism in the Town and Neighbourhood of Great Yarmouth*. London: John Kershaw, 1826.

Welford, Richard. *Men of Mark 'Twixt Tyne and Tweed*. Vol. 2. London: Walter Scott, 1895.

Wesley, John. *The Journal of the Rev John Wesley*. Vol. 3. Everyman's Library. London: J. M. Dent & Sons, 1906.

———. *A Short Account of the School in Kingswood, Near Bristol*. Bristol: William Pine, 1768.

White, William. *Emanuel Swedenborg: His Life and Writings*. London: Simpkin, Marshall, 1867.

Williams-Hogan, Jane. "A New Church in a Disenchanted World: A Study of the Formation and Development of the General Conference of the New Church in Great Britain." PhD diss., University of Pennsylvania, 1985.

www.ingramcontent.com/pod-product-compliance
Lightning Source LLC
LaVergne TN
LVHW020635100826
845148LV00012B/2192

9798385266616